Glory to God

"Gloria a Dios"

by

John Jacklin

A commissioned publication

23 Park Road, Ilkeston, Derbys DE7 5DA
Tel: 0115 932 0643 www.moorleys.co.uk

ISBN 978 086071 623 5

British Library Cataloguing in Publication Data.
A catalogue record for this book is available
from the British Library.

Printed from data supplied electronically

23 Park Road, Ilkeston, Derbys DE7 5DA
Tel: 0115 932 0643 www.moorleys.co.uk

Acknowledgements

I would like to give my very sincere thanks to Mary Reid, who gave me a great deal of advice, and Bob Lunt for their time editing the document, and Teresa Flowers who helped me with the first part.

*I wish to dedicate this book
to all my grandchildren and people,
of all ages, who will take time to read it.*

"For we are God's workmanship, created in Christ Jesus to do good works, which God prepared in advance for us to do"
Ephesians 2 v10

CONTENTS

FOREWORD

I was lucky – or should I say "blessed"? - to belong to the same lively Church youth group as John Jacklin. He was known to all of us as "Jacko" and I find it difficult to relate to him by any other name. "Jacko" was one of the central characters in our group – not because he was a ringleader but because he was a warm hearted, self-deprecating and deeply caring person. He viewed himself as a very "ordinary" person but he had a way of making "ordinary" rather special.

He was a touch accident-prone. We all used to go sailing on the Norfolk Broads every spring and Jacko had an unenviable reputation for falling in more than most. One of his greatest achievements was to have kept so relatively dry one year that he was able to lend some clothes to our curate who had been less successful in that department.

But there was another side to Jacko that not all of us saw at the time. He had a courageous faith and dogged commitment to his Lord. That commitment led him to walk away from the comfort of his surroundings and many friends and seek to serve Christ in South America. He went, not as a words person (although he proved himself to have gifts in that area), but with a builder's skills.

This book reveals the struggles he had to learn the language and find his place on a "mission field" more normally populated by preachers, teachers and nurses than builders. I am not convinced that his mission organisation really knew how to get the best out of a builder, but were not wrong to recognise his pastoral gifts and put those to work. His time with Ann and the growing family in Chile coincided with great social upheaval and times of uncertainty.

John writes with what at first appears to be a rambling style. He makes no pretence to be a "writer". On the other hand I found his rambles took me through interesting territory, and that territory includes a very honest revealing of his own hopes and disappointments. We also see the stresses that can be placed on missionary wives, and Ann comes out of these pages as someone who deserves a medal!

The great underlying theme is to give "Glory to God". In Chile, as I discovered when I was there for a mere fortnight, congregations can be lively and totally open about their joy as Christians. In John's life, and in particularly the hard-working years in Chile, God is clearly worth praising for the way he can guide and use "ordinary" people and do quite extraordinary things through them.

+ Gavin Reid

(Bishop of Maidstone 1992 – 2000).

INTRODUCTION TO CHILE

On the map Chile looks like a long runner bean. It has the Pacific Ocean on the west and the Andes Mountains dividing it from Argentina on the east. Chile is approximately 2,800 miles long, but never much more than 150 miles wide.

Chile is dry and hot in the north and has nitrates, copper, iron and other minerals, with the rainless Atacama Desert bordering on Peru. Chile's central region has a delightful Mediterranean climate. In the south the country has coal and lush forests with oilfields off Tierra del Fuego, where the weather can be wet and windy.

There is an abundance of all the fruit and vegetables that grow in temperate climates. Chile is a seafaring nation with rich fishing grounds, although the Humboldt Current makes the sea very cold.

Chile has a growing export industry, especially in fruit, fish, wine and timber. The capital Santiago is near the snow covered ski slopes of Portillo. In the south large forests, lakes and rivers provide excellent fishing and camping opportunities.

Chilean people are courteous, hospitable and generous, and appreciate jokes and witty conversation. They are naturally musical and often celebrate with dancing and song. The long hot summers enable people to eat alfresco and enjoy excellent national wines.

The Roman Catholic Church came to Chile during the Spanish conquest in the sixteenth century. Later more progressive priests and lay people founded orphanages, asylums, hospitals and schools.

The original inhabitants of Chile were Indians, but now the Mapuches (which means 'people of the land') remain. Some sources suggest that today they only number 400,000. They have their own language and culture and are mainly small farmers.

In 1894 the Araucanian (Anglican) Mission began with medical and educational work among the Mapuches and made known to them the Good News about Jesus. This has continued for over a hundred years.

Today there are many Anglican Churches in the Temuco region, and a growing number of Spanish-speaking Churches in Santiago and the cities of the north. Of course there are other denominations and the biggest of these is the Pentecostals, who make up 16.5% of the population.

INTRODUCTION

I was born in Blackheath in 1930 and grew up there during the war years in London. I had a wonderful childhood and have so much to thank my mum and dad for! Fortunately my grandparents, and most of my aunts and uncles, only lived within a few hundred yards from our home and I used to pop in to see them most days. Mum could be strict and used a small cane when necessary. Dad could be firm but I don't ever remember him smacking me. I lost over a year from school through illness, plus several months when we were bombed.

The Boys Brigade played a very important part in my life from the age of eleven to eighteen years old, giving me confidence, making me feel really valued and most importantly leading me to a personal faith in Jesus Christ. So I continue to have an extremely high regard for the Boys Brigade.

My dad worked as a foreman in a factory in Peckham. We never had too much money, but because I missed out on the eleven-plus exam my parents actually paid for me to go to Technical School. At least until the authorities realised my dad's wages were not high enough to pay the fees and fares. In my late teens I became involved in the Youth Club at St John's Church, Blackheath, helping me to mature mentally and spiritually and make many good friends, and one special friend, Ann Short, who was to become my wife in 1961.

Later the Lord enabled me to get through my building studies, and Ann and I were accepted to work in South America to carry out reconstruction work after an earthquake in Chile. People have said "What an interesting life you've had", and looking back that's absolutely true. I must therefore say that this has to be due to my parents and God's guidance. I have felt for some time it is extremely important that I tell this story because the Lord has done great things for us and we want him to get the credit and the praise. I felt the most appropriate title should be 'Gloria a Dios', for in Chile during worship services in the Pentecostal Churches people often spontaneously shout out these words when they feel God should be given the glory!

My hope and prayer is that through what's written here my grandchildren, and others who may read this book, will want to find out God's purpose for their lives too! Indeed this can be very difficult at times and is an on going process, but as an old lady in hospital once said to me, "You only have one life!" The old lady was, of course, right and it is therefore very important that we find out what the Lord wants us to do with our lives! I must also add it's always best to find out early in life, because it could save you a great deal of heartache later!

Chapter 1
EARLY CHILDHOOD AND GROWING UP

"I hear you're going to work in South America, are you going to work with an oil company?" I was in the doctor's surgery and had gone to ask him about my father's health. To my surprise he seemed quite enthused about my working in far away places. Dr Livingstone had known me since I was about three and a half, but I was rather at a loss to know how to answer his question. "Well I'm actually going to work for a missionary society!" I finally blurted out.

He was bending down at his desk and seemed to be struggling to get something out of a lower drawer. As I watched I could see the back of his neck gradually changing colour. Suddenly he looked up with eyes blazing and said, "Your father is going to die, you cannot go to South America!"

I had specifically wanted to discuss my dad's health with him so I was absolutely stunned by his reaction. His whole attitude had suddenly changed and he seemed to be extremely angry. Next, to my bewilderment, he stood up, and taking me by the elbow led along the corridor to open the front door of the surgery. Unexpectedly I found myself outside the surgery on the street with the front door shut behind me!

Sadly I was never to speak or to see Dr Livingstone again because within three years he was dead. Yet my father who had been so seriously ill, having had major surgery for cancer in 1956 removing the whole of his stomach, was to live for another twenty-two years!

My earliest childhood memories were of the flat my parents rented from a lovely Christian couple called Mr and Mrs Shepherd. It was part of their house and, if I remember correctly, we slept upstairs and had the use of the kitchen downstairs. Mr Shepherd was a deacon at the Baptist Church and got my father a job when dad came out of the Army after the first war. He was a skilled barge builder and I can still see him taking me into the garden, sitting me on a box and placing a hammer in my hand to bang nails into an upturned barrel. I was not quite three years old so my mother expressed some concern when she found out what we were doing. These were my first lessons in how to use a hammer, and I suppose created in me an early interest in making things with wood. I also remember Mr Shepherd made me a beautiful wheelbarrow – painted in several different colours - which I used as a push chair for my favourite teddy bear. Indeed one day having never been out on my own, I decided to take teddy for a walk. Going out through our front gate opposite Fossdene Road School I headed up to the shops. Discovering the gate open my mother was beside herself and frantically ran down the road asking if anyone had seen me. Very much out of breath she finally caught up with me as I was nearing the main road close to Charlton football ground. By this time the tears were running down my face – presumably because I realised I was lost - but to this day I have no idea why I really decided to venture out on my own at such a young age.

I was never punished as my mother was so grateful and relieved to find me. Later when I was five we moved up from Charlton to our own rented house at 44 Bowater Place, Blackheath. The doctor had in fact suggested my mother's health would be better away from the factories and nearer the clean air on the heath. The Shepherds' house in Fossdene Road only had a small back garden as Johnson & Phillips factory wall towered over it at the bottom. Some time after we had moved, all the neighbours who had lived in Fossdene Road were offered five pounds to move out, and all the houses were demolished to make room for the factory to be extended.

Soon after moving I began at Blackheath and Kidbrook School and enjoyed some very happy years there. The Head of the Infants department was Miss Bartlett, and my teacher was Miss Foster; both were very motherly. In the afternoon the younger children were expected to take a rest and lie down on fold up canvas beds in a darkened classroom with the curtains drawn. During one of the school's regular medical examinations we were all expected to strip down to our birthday suits. I don't remember why this was thought to be necessary but it was then that it was discovered that I had flat feet. I wasn't too bothered until I was ordered to march across the classroom starkers, and Miss Skinner, a school Governor and a regular churchgoer, called me 'Old flat feet'. She had no idea how miserable she made me feel and forever after I always gave her a wide berth - even later when I began to attend St John's Church! After the school medical I attended the Miller Hospital in Greenwich for electrical treatment twice a week, and had to wear leather supports in my shoes.

Before I was nine I became ill with Whooping Cough. Our family doctor advised my parents to take me away to Westgate-on-Sea to enable me to benefit from the sea air. Mum came with me and we stayed in a bed and breakfast for a whole year. Obviously dad couldn't come so he used to travel down by train at the weekends. As I began to improve, my parents would take me on long walks in the countryside and I clearly remember the fields of golden corn as harvest time was approaching.

In September 1939 we returned to London just before war against Germany (as Great Britain had promised to come to the aid of Poland if she was invaded). On the morning war was declared my parents arranged for a taxi to take us to Melksham, in Wiltshire. Aunt Edie, her son Bernard, mum and I were loaded into a warm taxi with some carrier bags of my most treasured toys and left London whilst it was still dark at five in the morning. I had never been in a taxi before, and certainly not to travel more than 100 miles! We were to stay with our relatives, Uncle Jack and Aunt Gladys, for my grandfather Clements (my mother's father) had originated from there. They had no children of their own but I really liked Uncle Jack. He was badly crippled as he had been wounded during the first war, and still had machine gun bullets and splinters of bone in his back. Despite this he was a master tailor and had his own business, with a large cutting room behind the shop. Aunt Gladys was also crippled with arthritis and in a wheelchair. This meant she was unable to get down the stairs so spent all of her time upstairs over the shop.

Mum allowed me to take about a hundred of my treasured toy soldiers, which I had painted yellow and wrapped individually in tissue paper and I used to play with them on Aunt Gladys's kitchen floor. Unfortunately it was here that I had my first test in gardening. From the kitchen window upstairs could be seen Uncle Jack's cutting room, and the garden below. One day Aunt Gladys asked me if I liked gardening. As hard as I try I really can't remember how I answered, but she decided I would be good at weeding! She was quite a formidable lady so I decided I would not go back upstairs to ask when I was unsure as to whether a plant was a weed or not. The rule I would work by was 'If in doubt pull it out!' In fact within two or three hours I felt it looked extremely tidy, although I must admit there were very few plants to be seen. Aunt Gladys, of course, wasn't able to jump up and down, but she certainly expressed her disapproval when she looked out of the window! It was then decided that very soon I was to be enrolled at the local school. However my cousin and I never really settled down and we only went there for a few weeks.

In the afternoons we would often go for long walks in the countryside to while away the time. I remember on one occasion we had been picking blackberries in the hedgerows, and as my mother clambered up the bank she tore a large hole in her stockings! As you may imagine stockings were almost impossible to buy during the war. Seeing the tear in my mother's precious hosiery my cousin and I immediately burst out laughing! We thought it was a huge joke, yet to my surprise my mother became absolutely furious and gave me a great ticking off. I was somewhat stunned by this, as my mother normally never went off like that. The incident still remains in my memory as I felt I had suffered a great injustice! It hurt most of all because my cousin had laughed as much as I did but his mother never said a word to him! In the end we felt so unwelcome and were all so homesick and unhappy that it was decided to return to London.

A year or so later I joined the Life Boys, which was the junior section of the Boys' Brigade. The lady in charge of Life Boys was Miss Wickes, and I especially remember she was assisted by Judy Mason whose father had founded our Boys' Brigade Company, and whose brothers served as officers. Judy later left to join the Royal Navy as a Wren Officer, and kept in touch with me over the years, calling me 'One of her boys!' A little while before my twelfth birthday I was allowed to join the 2nd West Kent (Blackheath) Company of the Boys' Brigade.

The Blitz

The first part of the war was extremely quiet until the Blitz started. Then during the 1940's in London there were air raids every night. My dad often used to stay at work overnight at the paper factory in Peckham. He was taking turns with others in 'Fire Watching' because the factory had a glass roof and was very vulnerable to the German incendiary bombs. Dad also joined the London Defence Volunteers, which later became incorporated into the Home Guard. He had been a soldier in the first war and feeling he must do his part joined with others, many of whom had no military experience: I used to watch them drill on Blackheath at the weekends. At this early stage they had no uniforms and only a few rifles, so some had to drill with broomsticks! On other nights dad would be called out to guard such things as unexploded bombs until they could be dealt with.

Most nights, however, we would be together in our Anderson Shelter covered with two or three feet of earth, at the bottom of our garden. In the shelter we could clearly hear the screeching, screaming, whistling of the bombs as they sped through the air. One night as they got closer I remembered someone had said: 'If you get a direct hit you'll never hear it!' Eventually on this night there was such an almighty explosion. After what seemed a long a pause came the noise of earth and debris all falling down on top of our shelter! I was quite excited and immediately wanted to rush outside to have a look! My father in his great wisdom, however, told me to stay inside for a bit, for soon the very strong acrid fumes made it hard to breathe, and they were stinging our eyes! A bomb had fallen about six feet from our shelter in the next door's garden! Fortunately it had fallen in soft earth, so apart from knocking down the fence and uprooting several large shrubs, plus breaking panes of glass in the windows it caused no serious damage. Eventually I scrambled out of the Anderson to see the crater which was about eight feet across. Our neighbours had already moved away as an earlier bomb had destroyed half their house following a direct hit that completely demolished the baker's shop on the corner.

I remember previously going through the rubble of the corner shop and finding things like tins of shoe polish and laces. Thinking these to be the spoils of war and really of no value to the original owners I took the goods proudly to my mother saying, 'Look what I found, Mum'. To my surprise she wasn't impressed, and gave me the money and sent me up the road to pay the baker's wife who now lived in an adjacent street. There was still a great deal of dignity and sense of right and wrong even though there was a war going on. Behind the shop there was a bake house where Mr Richards had his oven. At one time I used to work in the bake house on Saturday mornings, one of my principal jobs being to paint the bread rolls with a mixture of egg, sugar and warm water. This made them come out of the oven all golden and shiny, and the smell of newly baked bread really got my taste buds going. A tradition that still persisted was that on Sundays, and especially at Christmas time, housewives would bring their joints, chickens or turkeys to be cooked in the large baker's oven.

Occasionally I would go out on the bread rounds delivering bread, but I could never push a bread barrow as these were far too heavy for me.

Isolation Ward

At some stage during the Blitz Uncle Ted's (my dad's younger brother's) children used to come to stay overnight with us, as their dad was an Air Raid Warden always on duty at night. As there were too many of us to stay in the Anderson Shelter in the garden we all slept downstairs on mattresses on the living-room floor. During this time I unfortunately developed a high fever and a very red sore throat, although I don't remember feeling very ill. After some days off school the family doctor decided to take some swabs and it was diagnosed that I had diphtheria. It was January 1941 in the middle of the blitz and I had the distinction of being the only child in the whole of the Borough of Greenwich to have this honour. The authorities were very fearful that now, in the second year of the war in the midst of ferocious daily air bombardments, they might have to cope with a diphtheria epidemic as well! Unfortunately because of the danger of infection my cousins could no longer stay with us at night. My parents had to go for tests and dad had to stay off work until the results came through that fortunately showed they were clear. Almost immediately I found myself being rushed to the Brook Fever Hospital opposite Woolwich Common. I can still remember the ambulance coming to the house, and the gaggle of neighbours standing around our front door, as I was taken out swathed in blankets on a stretcher.

The German Luftwaffe still continued to visit us every night meeting out their demonic destruction, devastating everything around with no pity for either people or property! Their aircraft were not aiming at military targets, but just continuing their satanic schemes to destroy the morale of the people of London! As I look back I find it almost unbelievable as I remember seeing street after street of rubble, which only a few hours before had been people's homes. Night after night these merciless bombings continued to pulverise so many of the large warehouses and factories along the Thames. Often the burnt-out buildings were left as just smoking shells in the morning with only the outer walls standing. During these night raids many buildings blazed like mighty furnaces with an incredible orange glow started by the incendiary bombs. One night as we gazed across the Thames the whole of the north bank seemed to be ablaze! Silver Town and the area including Tate and Lyle's sugar factory was on fire, just like

16

some gigantic fireworks display, making the Royal Fireworks look more like a child's bonfire celebration!

My first few days in the Brook Hospital were very lonely in the isolation ward; I didn't understand what was going on and time passed very slowly. Fortunately, in just over a week I was moved out of this ward and events suddenly moved fast. It was quickly decided that I was less infectious and I was moved to a ward full of wounded soldiers back from the evacuation of Dunkirk. As an only child I had felt especially lonely being away from my parents for the first time; likewise I knew my mum and dad were missing me a great deal. However, every morning the nurse would bring me a packet of Beanos and other comics to read. My dad had called by and handed these to the porter on duty at the gate, because I was not allowed any visitors whatsoever in a fever hospital. I later discovered that everything I touched had been incinerated afterwards for fear of infection.

One night when we were all in bed there was such an almighty explosion that a large timber beam fell down inside the entrance to our ward. In the morning we were told that a house in the hospital grounds had taken a direct hit, and two doctors had been blown to pieces. Another night during bombing the sergeant in the next bed bellowed at me "Lad get out and get under your bed," and then he did the same! Gradually, although I was still missing my parents, a wonderful thing was happening, for those wounded soldiers had actually started to become my family! They taught me how to play darts and draughts, and loved to carry me around on their shoulders. I was eleven years old and was suddenly being adopted by a whole ward of soldiers! They were obviously missing their families as well! Surprisingly, I have to say, the food in hospital was really fantastic! There were jellies and blancmanges, cakes and sticky buns and the things you just couldn't get because of the food rationing. There were masses of eggs, and one night I actually ate six boiled eggs and really got myself constipated! Yet I still continued to be homesick and on some nights slipped out onto a flat roof to see the best way to escape.

One night it had been snowing quite a bit and I rolled up a couple of snowballs, throwing them as far as I could. Looking across the flat snow-covered roofs I could see part of the boundary wall had been destroyed by a bomb. 'Surely I could slip through there, and then there's only about two miles walk to get home?' I thought to myself.

Yes, there was a possible way of escape, but with snow on the ground I finally decided against it! Time seemed to pass extremely slowly again and as each day came and went I began to wonder if I would ever see my home again. Then almost without warning I was finally discharged and sent home; presumably my diphtheria had not been that serious!

Destruction and Death

Back home the bombing continued, but not so intensively, so we moved back into the house to sleep in the warmth and comfort of our own beds upstairs. Although we had received two near misses we had no idea the worst was still to come. The calm was to be all too short-lived and one night I woke up in the middle of the night to hear my dad calling me. As I opened my eyes everything was pitch black and then, putting up my hand, I discovered I was under my bed on the floor! 'Be careful as you come out' dad said, and then I found there was broken glass all over the floor. My dressing table mirror had been smashed. Looking up, I realized I was looking at the sky, as there was no ceiling or roof over us! We quickly went downstairs, carefully picking our way through the debris, and soon the short night was over. There had been a large bomb dropped in the next street, one of the very heavy ones that came down on two green parachutes. Most of our roof had been blown off but a large part was still supported by the jagged end of one of the rafters. To my great astonishment this piece of timber was embedded in my mattress like some giant sword, just about where my stomach had been! By the grace of God I had been snatched out of bed and pushed underneath it!

Sadly we discovered the news was very bad. The whole of the next street had been completely destroyed, and my cousin George whom I sat next to at school was dead. He had been trapped under the rubble and gassed from the fumes of a broken gas pipe. His father had lost an eye and the whole family was utterly devastated. George and his brother Reg had both been in the Boys' Brigade with me and later the whole family decided to emigrate to Australia and begin a new life there.

My parents and I then went to live a few houses away at 34 Lizban Street, with Aunt Helen, my mother's sister. This was the house my grandparents had lived in, where from the front upstairs bedrooms you could look over into the Rectory Field which was the sports ground belonging to Blackheath Cricket and Rugby Club. Once again I stayed away from school – until after three months my mother decided I should think about going back.

School of Building

Presumably because I had already lost so much time away from school with whooping cough and later diphtheria I was never entered for the eleven-plus exam. My parents therefore decided to enter me for the entrance exam for the notable LCC School of Building at Brixton (one of the early Technical Schools). When we were bombed out I was still only in my first year at my new school, so after three months away from school mum arranged an interview and went with me to see the Headmaster. I told Mr Dowsett that I would soon be fourteen; I didn't want to come back to school but wanted to go to work. He was an extremely strict man with the reputation of being able to make the boys cry just by talking to them! Although soon I was to realise he was a much wiser man than I had given him credit for he said, 'Well if you don't come back, what sort of job do you think you'll get?' This rather put me on the back foot and I didn't quite know how to answer. Then he added 'Well, I will tell you, you will get a job sweeping the floor for a few shillings a week and you won't get very far!' Then treating me as an adult he said, 'But that's up to you, you must make up your own mind!' So I returned home and puzzled over things for several days; it was the hardest decision I had been expected to make so far, but finally it seemed to be sensible to return to school. I see now the Lord was obviously guiding me, although I didn't realise that at the time. I need here to include a great expression of thanks to my parents for sending me to the School of Building at Brixton, and being really concerned for my education.

Dad working in a factory as a charge hand, (i.e. a working foreman) made a considerable sacrifice when they decided to send me to what was at that time a fee-paying school. Wonderfully, though, within that first year it was decided that my dad did not earn enough to pay my fees, and so from then on no further fees were paid. Even better still the education authority decided to pay my parents a monthly allowance to cover my bus fares and other expenses. The journey took one and a half hours across London and meant taking three separate buses.

I would catch a number 53 bus from Charlton Road to New Cross, then sometimes take a 40 tram to Camberwell Green, and finally a 4a bus to Brixton. Travelling on the tram was quite an experience. As these vehicles got up speed the older trams would sway from side to side and the woodwork would creak! The double-deckers carried 54 passengers and I would often meet up with some of the lads from Greenwich who could be found playing cards near the front on the top deck. Occasionally if a lad had a bad hand of cards he would throw them all out of the window! I normally travelled with Graham who had also taken the entrance exam with me and lived quite near.

The lads in my year at Technical School were quite an interesting bunch. One boy, called Wasserman, was a Polish Jew and very good at maths and physics. He was a very quiet boy, but sometimes he would help me with my maths homework. Other boys had previously been to Grammar School and were much brighter than I was. However there was a good atmosphere and we all generally got on well together. Talking about the boys from Greenwich, two of them, English and Hawkins, were what we called 'Wide Boys' - what we would call street wise today! English always dressed in expensive suits, had lots of money, and a shock of wavy blonde hair. Hawkins used to play in goal for the school, until the day he had an accident in the wood cutting machine shop and chopped two of his centre fingers off! You can imagine that following the initial shock there were all sorts of stories about boys raking through the shavings to see who could find the missing fingers! These two lads from Greenwich were always stealing things. Hawkins used to come to school with a small suitcase containing his exercise books and drawing instruments. This was very useful for removing stuff from school, namely lead ingots, brass, copper and other metals from the plumbing shop, which he could sell nearer home as scrap metal. Sometimes his case was almost too heavy to carry to the bus stop! At other times he would remove the screws from the stock of a tee square, put it in his pocket and then push the wooden blade down inside his trouser leg to enable him to get it out of school. At one stage these two 'Wide Boys' had several spare lockers jammed full with other boys set squares and drawing instruments. That is until one day when some of our class decided to ransack these lockers, and forcing open the doors let dozens and dozens of personal utensils cascade onto the corridor floor! Hawkins and English could obviously not report this to the Headmaster as all these things were stolen goods!

During 1943 a new Education Act made it compulsory for all schools to teach Religious Knowledge. This was difficult for some teachers, who felt this was a subject for which they had little experience, or for which they had little conviction for. On the other hand it brought the Christian staff out of the woodwork. A teacher called Mr Parry got us learning some of Jesus' parables off by heart. One week we were expected to memorise Jesus' story of the 'Pharisee and the Tax Collector.' As we recited this passage one lad got a bit mixed up and quoted the Pharisee as praying 'God, I thank thee that I am not as other men are, unjust, adulterers, and contortionists.' At once the whole class dissolved into laughter as we pictured this man twisting and swinging his body around all over the place! The word he should have used was 'extortionist', certainly these classes were far from boring and we had great fun. During the morning break we were allowed out of school, usually congregating in "Aida's" sweet shop on the corner across the road. Here sitting on the crates of bottles we would consume sticky buns, cream slices or cheesecakes with coconut on top, and bottles of fizzy drink. Aida was a gentle, generous old lady, but some of the boys waited until she turned round to reach something on the shelf, to pinch sweets out of the large jars on the front of the counter!

I coped with school dinners for the first year. However on the staircase going up to Maths I found the smell of cooked cabbage so vile that I wanted to vomit, and it put me off school meals completely. Graham and I therefore decided to run all the way down Ferndale Road to Woolworth's in Brixton Road. Here they were selling hot sausages in bread rolls, so we used our dinner money to pay for them, and then ran all the way back to school! After about six weeks however I began to get a lot of stomach pains and mum took me to see Dr Livingstone. 'Do they have school dinners at your school?' he asked me. I was able to say yes, they did. However then he said, 'But what about you, do you eat school dinners?', and I had to confess I didn't! 'This boy is suffering from chronic indigestion', he told my mother, and insisted that what I needed was a school dinner each day. Sadly I then had to eat the ghastly school dinners until I left school! Some years later I did actually buy a cooked meal there in the evenings, when I returned to do my Higher National at night school. However the food had then improved a bit, but I only ate it as there was no other option!

Graham and I were both in the Boys' Brigade, and our mothers had been friends for many years since their school days. We continued to go by bus until in my last year at school and then we went by bicycle. Dad had said if I could save half the cost of a bicycle they would pay the rest. Consequently I got an early morning paper round before going to school and began saving hard, so that within a year I was able to buy a brand new B.S.A. bicycle. I always remember that it was one of the first coloured ones, and was a bright turquoise. Until that time all bikes manufactured during the war had to be black. Once on our bicycles Graham and I could get to school in about half the time, using all the back streets around Camberwell and Herne Hill, and my parents allowed me to keep the bus fare as pocket money. Of course in those days the traffic was nowhere as busy as it is now. On the other hand there more buses, sometimes with three, four or even five following each other. That was in addition to the old trams as well. I mention this because between the tram lines was a centre rail which was very deep and on several occasions we got a bicycle wheel jammed in this. The bicycle wheel would go down up to the axle, which tended to throw you off into the road. Despite this neither of us had any serious injuries, due to the grace of God and good tram drivers.

During the first year at the School of Building in Brixton we spent two periods a week in one of the seven different workshops, changing at the end of each month. Workshops included brick-work, carpentry and joinery, painting and decorating, plastering, plumbing, masonry, and wood cutting machinery. The second year I decided to specialise in carpentry and joinery. We also had theory classes in building plus all our normal academic subjects. I never excelled in geometry so during exams I used to work out most of the answers by trigonometry. Before I went to Brixton our school gymnasium had been destroyed by a fire during the Blitz, so we had to use a church Hall down the road, although we were allowed do physical exercises on the school roof, as this was enclosed with a large wire cage. At least most of it was - except there were some parts with gaping holes in. This presented a great challenged to certain of my peers who would specifically try to throw the ball though the holes! I suppose this was like playing basketball without the baskets. If these boys were successful the ball would pass through the hole, falling several storeys below, finally bouncing between the unsuspecting and startled members of the public down in the street! Remarkably, no one ever got hurt and enthusiastic volunteers were always ready to speed down several flights of stairs to retrieve the ball from Ferndale Road! Anything for a diversion as this delayed the class and made these boring periods much livelier! I left school in July 1947 and worked under the Greater London Council's apprenticeship scheme in the building industry until 1951.

Boys' Brigade Camps

In 1942 just before I was twelve I attended my first Boys' Brigade annual camp under canvas. During the war we camped for several years on Agar's Plough, which was part of the famous playing fields of Eton College. Having never been on holiday on my own I began to get homesick, added to which I had stomach ache and diarrhoea. Soon, however, I discovered the care and concern of the Rev Tony Waite, our Chaplain and Vicar of St John's Blackheath, and Mr Ben Porter who was Captain of the 14th West Kent (Bexleyheath) Company. Both of these men took it in turns to bring me tea and arrowroot biscuits in the mornings whilst the other boys were having breakfast. The senior boys, especially our Tent Commander, were very caring in looking after the younger boys - although there were two older boys who made my existence a misery, but I suppose that's life!

There were about ten of us to a tent. At 6.30 each morning everyone had to go over to the open air enclosure and wash in cold water. Then we progressed to a large wooden building where breakfast was cooked and served. The meals were always very good. Following breakfast we had tent inspection when a member of staff came round to inspect our folded blankets and straw mattresses. We were allowed to dress in shirt and shorts, but our shoes, brass buckles and leather belts all had to be cleaned, polished and placed on display. Swimming parade then followed when we would all go down to the open-air swimming pool belonging to Eton College. This was really part of a backwater off the Thames and fish used to swim around us in the deeper part. In the afternoons there were sports competitions between tents and the different companies in the London District. At night we all had a cup of hot cocoa, and our Tent Commander led prayers.

We were allowed to go rowing on the Thames under supervision and on one afternoon during the week to go shopping in Windsor. Once about eight of us all managed to use the Public Toilet in Windsor by keeping the door open, and just using one penny! The open-air loos in camp were O.K. but we preferred the luxury of flushing toilets and a lift up seat! The Sunday Church Parade was always a very impressive occasion when several hundred boys, including the London District, and Slough and District bands, all marched along the main road to a morning service in Eton College Chapel. I continued to go to summer camp every year for seven years as a boy and then for three years as Staff Sergeant. Being Sports Officer was very demanding, organising competitions and refereeing, so that by the end of the week I was exhausted and tried to take a holiday. Yet it was very fulfilling and I would not have wanted it any other way.

Coming to Personal Faith

The greatest thing the Boys' Brigade ever did for me was to bring me to know Jesus personally when I was thirteen years old. This was very much due to the extremely caring attitude of my Squad Commander. Dennis Peterson was in charge of my Squad, and when I was ill he would call round to visit me. White haversacks were part of our uniform, but being wartime it was difficult to get the brass button. Dennis even went to the trouble of actually making one for me, so I always had a high regard for him. We had a club each Saturday, and during the break one evening Dennis asked me if I wanted to become a Christian. Around that time one or two others like David Able and Bill Clarke had make their decision to follow Christ. Although I hadn't felt any need to do so, I saw no reason why I shouldn't. My decision was nothing dramatic, but unknown to me it was obviously going to make a big difference to my whole life in the future.

On becoming a Christian I saw that certain things had to change in my life, such as dirty stories, which the boys always seemed to laugh at, and swearing, both of these needed to be left out. I still think the Boys' Brigade is the best youth organisation. The Founder, Sir William Smith, a committed Christian, began the Brigade in Glasgow on Thursday 4th October 1883. It was the first uniformed organisation for boys, and much later to include girls, and can still be found all over the world. Baden Powell was a great friend of William Smith, and was later inspired to start the Boy Scouts as he saw the Boys' Brigade met a tremendous need amongst the young people of its day. Some feel because of that the B.B. and its founder should be given more credit. However for me the Boys Brigade is by far the more important of the two organisations because its objective is 'The advance of Christ's kingdom among boys'.

At one stage our Company had Royal Marine Sergeants take us for gymnastics. They were on the staff of the Royal Naval College at Greenwich training Naval Officers. When I first started gym I could never jump over the box horse – for in those days springboards were never used! Because of this Sergeant Lung called me 'the strange boy', but later I became really good at vaulting, and won badges for Gymnastics and First Aid. I also enjoyed football and cricket, but I was never very good at swimming, although I did get a certificate. I had a go at learning to play the kettledrum, but failed the first test and decided not to continue. One thing I used to do quite well at was athletics, especially the sprints and high and long jumps. On the negative side I make no secret of the fact that I never really enjoyed drill, especially when I was made Lance Corporal and was expected to give orders. Squad drill wasn't too bad, and my squad won the Company Squad Drill competition medal several times. It was the big Battalion and London District drill competitions that scared me, when I always preferred to stay in the ranks even after I became a Sergeant! During these competitions my mind would go blank when expected to give commands. Fortunately, Roger Mercer who was over six feet tall was the right hand man standing next to me. When my mind went blank Roger would whisper the words of command into my ear.

Today I still have to confess that I preferred to be in the ranks! Yet even these events could be fun especially when Sid Mew, one of our officers, discovered one tall lad had turned up wearing one black shoe

Brighton beach 1948 with Chum Wolf,
Fred Ashby and myself.

Battalion Drill Competition at Woolwich 1949

and one brown one! A huge laugh really but we had a crisis. Then with great initiative Sid immediately made the boy take his shoes off and exchanged them for his own. Fortunately the officer happened to have the same size! The second most important thing the B.B. gave me was a sense of self-worth. Each member was important and valued, and most of the competitions were planned in such a way that the squad or team depended upon every person participating, no matter how small or new or inexperienced you might be!

I had become a Christian when I was thirteen, and later when I was seventeen I began classes to prepare for Confirmation. On Saturday evenings candidates would attend classes at the old Vicarage

(eventually sold to become the local library in St John's Park), when the Rev Martin Parsons was Vicar. Each week we would come away with a sheet of paper with about twenty questions

Easter Boys Brigade Camp at Fairseat Kent 1949

26

which had to be answered before the next session. I used to take these classes seriously, but when my sheet was returned to me it inevitably had more red ink on it than anyone else's! I became so discouraged although I knew I was a Christian. Eventually I decided that because I couldn't give the right academic answers I would give it all up! Kneeling down at my bedside one night I had decided to pray for the last time. Later I spoke to Mr Parsons about my decision, yet to my surprise he said he didn't want me to give things up, saying the written answers weren't the most important part. So in the end I was confirmed at St Margaret's, Lee, with the other members of the class.

In my last year as a boy in the Company I was given an award for being in command of the squad that won the annual Squad Drill Competition. The prize was a book on the life of Dr David Livingstone, and one that has left its mark on my life. It was not so much his time in Africa, but the determined way he got down to his studies to get into medical school that impressed me. David was born on Clydeside and as the book says 'came from the godly poor', living in a tenement close to the factory where his father worked. David was always up at 5.30 am and after a brief breakfast of porridge went straight to work as a mill hand in the factory. At 8.00 pm he finished work and then attended night school for another two hours. He would then come home and often still be studying at midnight until his mother insisted he put his candle out! His hard work eventually gained him a place at Anderson's college, a prominent medical school in Glasgow. His grit and determination still continue to inspire me!

St John's and 3 Johns!

Towards the end of my time in the Boys' Brigade I began to attend the King's Own Youth Fellowship at St John's on Sunday evenings. Several boys from the Company used to go and I also found a lot of new friends there. At this time I began to go sailing on the Norfolk Broads cruises after Easter with the Youth Fellowship, organised by Charlie Cope our Commodore, with Gavin Reid as Vice Commodore.

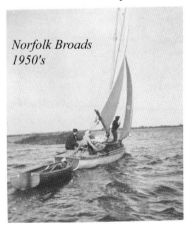

Norfolk Broads 1950's

Myself, John Dubbey, John Hollingsworth (later to be my best man), Philip Akhurst and Cecil Broughton went on several holidays together. We were really indebted to John Dubbey on the Scottish holiday because at that stage he was the only one who had a car and a driving licence! When we three Johns and Philip arrived at a Christian Guest House in Edinburgh, we were asked our names so I said we were 'I John, II John, III John and Revelation'!

Dennis Peterson

I also enjoyed several Christian Youth holidays in Swanage, Southern Ireland, and North Wales. We had great fun several years in Kilkee, a Christian Endeavour Guest House in Southern Ireland, sometimes slipping out early in the morning to bodily lift the cars, between the four of us, pushing them so tight together that the drivers couldn't get out! I have usually found a sense of humour to be quite useful,

Hauled up the mast upside down.

but I will not mention too many incidents. Some of these have caused embarrassment to Ann and on occasions she has said 'the trouble with you is that everyone doesn't appreciate your sense of humour'. It's true and one year on the Norfolk Broads two of the blokes, namely John D. Smith and John Willie Smith, retaliated by taking me by the feet and hoisting me up the mast upside down. We had many marvellous times together and there are so many other friends I could mention. I trust they will forgive me therefore, if I do not mention them all by name. Indeed when we meet now and again

Walking to morning service on the Broads, Ann second from right at front.

for reunions there are still more than a hundred of us who are former members of St John's Youth Fellowships!

Scottish Holiday with John Dubbey, Philip Ackhurst and John Hollingsworth. 1950's

Scottish Holiday – John Hollingsworth 1950's

The Army Experience

Conscription into the Armed Forces was still compulsory, but if you were a student or apprentice you could get a deferment. Actually if I had done my National Service when eighteen I would have only done 18 months, but the government decided to increase it to two years by the time I was twenty one! I applied for the Navy, but finally went into the Army and had to report to the REME Training Camp at Blandford in Dorset. A lot of the lads in my intake had been apprentices, and others had been at university. Six weeks' basic training seemed like a very long sentence especially when you were in Sergeant Andrews' platoon. Apparently he had come out of the Army at the end of the war and set up a small business selling motorcycles in Scotland. Unfortunately for him, and us, the venture failed and he decided to come back into the Army! On the train journey down to Dorset I experienced my first misfortune when my front crown came off. This meant I couldn't drink or eat anything hot or very cold for almost a week. Army procedure insisted that I had to report sick to see the dentist. This took up some time and I missed several sessions of drill and arms training.

Several lads in my barrack room reckoned they were Christians but they showed no inclination to pray or go to Church so I went on my own one Sunday morning. Seeing I was new the Chaplain said 'Come and have a chat', so one day I went along to see him during the dinner hour. Returning to the barrack room I was confident I was in good time for the very important Company Sergeant Major's parade that afternoon. Yet it seemed strange that our barrack room was empty; however, I went straight to my locker for my rifle. Leaving the room I glanced up at the blackboard just to check the time – when to my astonishment I found all the afternoon's activities had been rubbed off! Suddenly it dawned on me that everyone was already outside somewhere. Rushing up to the main parade ground I found our platoon on the Square! Trying unsuccessfully to attract Sergeant Andrews' attention, and as time seemed to be of the essence, I ran onto the Square. Almost immediately I became aware of a booming voice echoing all around me bellowing "Get that man off the Square!" I didn't quite understand why I was not supposed to go onto the Square, as no one had explained this part of army tradition! Later it was explained to me that "The Square" is holy ground, especially to Sergeant Majors, and must be treated with great reverence! At this point I looked across to Sergeant Andrews, thinking he would surely be pleased to see me. Unfortunately he seemed to be having some sort of a seizure, as his face had turned purple and he had difficulty getting his words out! Later I discovered that he was beside himself because one of his recruits had actually arrived late for the Company Sergeant Major's parade! Suddenly he was overwhelmed with a great sense of shame; he would never be the same sergeant again.

That evening I was summoned to the corporal's office where the two corporals and Sergeant Andrews were waiting to see me. I tried hard to explain that I had got back in good time for parade, had checked the programme on the blackboard and found this had been cleaned and the times rubbed out. Sergeant Andrews would not listen to me, and beside himself with anger accused me of going to see the Padre to report him for swearing! This was of course a complete fabrication and just a smoke screen. What he was really incensed about was that I had embarrassed him by turning up late for the Sergeant Major's parade that afternoon. My punishment for this was that I was being dropped from the passing out parade! By this time tears were running down my face. I had never reported him for swearing and although this upset me, I just couldn't cope with the bullying way he treated us. Later the corporals told us that Sergeant Andrews wasn't the monster he appeared to be! He was really joking when he went into a rage, and after ticking us all off and leaving the barrack room, he would often burst out laughing!

Most of us were mature twenty one year olds, and we worked extremely hard every night up to lights out cleaning our equipment in the barrack room. Then after eleven o'clock we continued bulling our boots in the wash place until you could see your face in them! We were a very dedicated crowd and could never be accused of shirking! Every night we were working until to the early hours, and then up again at six in the morning. This meant we would often find ourselves nodding forward, fighting to keep awake during weapons training. Later I was called to see the young lieutenant in charge of our company who asked me how I was getting on and how I found Sergeant Andrews. I really just didn't want to say anything against the Sergeant so I just said 'Well he has a job to do.' At this stage, however, I had no idea of the bad reports that had been getting through about Sergeant Andrews, and some months on he was posted to Japan. I also discovered later that several recruits in the camp had committed suicide whilst on basic training!

Before leaving the camp I had an interview with the Personnel Officer, a very affable major, who invited me to sit down and offered me a cigarette. He suggested that because I was reasonably intelligent I could be trained as an Armourer which was an 'A' class trade, but I decided I would do the shortest course possible and become an Army Clerk which was only a class 'B' trade.

After basic training, and a Clerk's Course in Gosport, I was eventually posted to REME Ack Ack Group Workshops at Woolwich, behind Charlton Park, for the next eighteen months. On reflection I sometimes wonder if the Army was trying to make it up to me following my experience with Sergeant Andrews. It now meant I was able to live at home and commute to the camp on Woolwich Common each day, except when I was on guard or had some duty, and was able to worship at St John's Church on most Sundays.

'Mountaineering'

During this time I met Tommy Morgan, our new Curate, who had recently been demobbed after serving as a Major in the Indian Army. Shortly afterwards he asked me to help with "Mountaineers" a new Bible Class on Sunday mornings. I soon discovered Tommy was a wonderful encourager and we struck up a great friendship. I especially remember the day he asked me to call at his digs and pray with him, something I had always found very hard to do. So when Tommy suggested we pray out loud I was very embarrassed and was not at all happy. Yet since then I have always been extremely grateful to Tommy for teaching me how to pray out loud, and have found it to be very important when trying to help people. Tommy would also lend me books and commentaries, and sometimes his own notes. Later he became ill and gave me quite a lot of his theological books, one or two of which I still have, although when his health improved I insisted he have most of them back again. "Mountaineers" were quite a mixed bunch and a great challenge. A few came from good homes, but others came from less privileged families. I remember two brothers who came from a large family whose mother had left home. Often they would turn up late, or not at all, and this was frequently because their father had sent them out shopping or insisted they had to have a bath! Tommy and I spent quite a lot of time trying to help this family as the father found it difficult to cope after his wife left him. In theory three of us led the Bible Class, two brothers and I, together with the lady who kindly played the piano. Most of the time however Miss Claridge and I were on our own whilst the other two leaders were away at university. Later she had to resign to look after her elderly mother, and this was where I teamed up with my future wife! I called to see Ann at her home knowing she played the piano to ask if she could possibly be brave enough to help us. Discipline could be extremely difficult with the boys playing all sorts of tricks, and sometimes hurling missiles across the room whilst the class was in progress! I can still see Ann crouched over the piano expecting a hymn book, or some other missile, to hit her from behind at any moment! I would usually arrive in good time at the hall, which was always warm as Emily Parsons, our Vicar's wife, would have been there before me to prepare to light the stove. At first I didn't know who actually did this kindness.

She didn't have to do this but was a very caring, motherly person with three children of school age, and would do such things without drawing attention to herself. One morning, arriving early and about to enter the hall, I found the door partly open and realised the boys had set a trap for me. Fortunately before going in I noticed that a bucket of cold water had been carefully balanced on the top of the door, ready to pour its contents all over me as I entered! On previous occasions they had done similar tricks with a pile of heavy books, but I accepted such things as all part of the fun!

Missionary Challenge

At the beginning of the early 1950's the "Twenty Plus" group felt it would be a great idea to start an annual young people's weekend away. After consultation it was decided this could be held at "Foxbury" the Church Missionary Society's training college in Chislehurst in Kent, whist the students were on holiday. Although the weekend was for young people, to give it a bit of stability Harvey and Maimie Cantrell were asked to be house parents. They had been missionaries in Kenya for many years and were now living in Blackheath. They were a great couple; Harvey had been an engineer and was very down to earth. Maimie was a very warm and generous Scottish lady. These weekends were always full of fun, with some practical jokes, a tennis tournament, and talks given by guest speakers. Ann celebrated her twenty-first birthday on one of these weekends, her friends made her a cake, and I embarrassed her by buying her a see-through nylon blouse with an Elizabethan collar and a Cruden's Concordance!

One weekend we had a speaker who had been a missionary in China. This lady fitted the traditional image I had always had of a rather serious looking person, dressed in a rather drab outfit, and of course wearing a hat! However, she soon completely shattered that image as she began to speak. Immediately her whole face became radiant with a beautiful smile and we were transfixed with her words. She told us of a couple called John and Betty Stam who were missionaries in China in the 1930's during the civil war there. The Communists were utterly ruthless in their treatment of the missionaries and the couple were taken out and beheaded. Unbeknown to their captors the Stams had a small daughter who was left in the house. Mercifully friends later found the little girl and took her to look after. As our speaker continued I found myself weeping uncontrollably, and I had to slip out of the chapel into the grounds on that beautiful summer afternoon. Some of my friends became concerned and asked me what was wrong. At that stage I found it difficult to explain what was happening. Later however I came to realise that I had felt challenged by this couple who were prepared to die because of their love for Jesus. Even today this experience continues to influence me and challenge me in the way in which I spend my life! Each year at our 'Foxbury' weekend the tennis tournament was inevitably won by our Vicar John Preston - he was good at everything! We also used to have some good rambles and formed many lasting friendships as we went for walks in the Kent countryside together.

On-going Training

During the second year of my National Service, and being posted at Woolwich, I began to wonder if it might be possible to continue my building studies at the Polytechnic. Speaking to my boss, Captain Gale, I found him very sympathetic, and he gave me Wednesday off each week to attend the Polytechnic and complete my National Certificate in Building. I finished my Army Service at the end of my college course and here things worked out in such a way that I could never have imagined! During the last term the students were taken to visit a large modern brick works in Bedfordshire. After the visit Mr Everson, Head of the Building Department at the Poly, asked me what I intended to do when I came out of the Army? I had to say I wasn't really sure, but didn't want to go back to my old job. He then explained that a Mr Kenneth Miller, manager of the company's Estates and Planning Department, needed a draughtsman to work at their London office. I confided in Mr Everson that I was not at all confident I could do the job, but he assured me that they would train me, and he would recommend me on the strength of my college work. Here I must express my sincere thanks to Mr Everson for his tremendous support. Indeed he not only built up my confidence, he actually lent me his own expensive set of drawing instruments to start my new job! At first I worked with seventeen others in a large drawing office, but later finished up in my own small office. I enjoyed being at Eastwood's where the work included designing houses, depot buildings, and even a new cricket pavilion. Sometimes I would go out on site to assist the surveyors, and sometimes I went on my own. Later I was asked to be secretary to the small Christian Union, and found there were several active Christians on the staff. From time to time we were given permission to use the company's boardroom for special meetings, and were able to show a series of Fact and Faith films to which the Company Secretary and other Directors came.

Our Assistant Managing Director, Mr Paisley was a Christian and a member of the Plymouth Brethren. During the Billy Graham campaigns in London he made his large grey Rolls Royce available, complete with peaked capped-driver, to take people to Haringey Arena. It still makes me smile to think that later, when he became Managing Director, he annoyed the directors by prohibiting the consumption of whiskey and cigars at board meetings! Mr Paisley was a very committed Christian and once or twice actually came to our Christian Union meetings In fact one week when the speaker didn't turn up he gave the address and spoke on "You must be born again!" On Saturday afternoons I played football for the firm, and was

Colleagues at Rangers House
Blackheath mid 1950's

elected vice captain. My life was now extremely busy, studying most nights at Brixton to get my Higher National. On Sunday afternoons I would visit old people in nursing homes with members of the Youth Fellowship, and in the evenings helped lead the "Twenty Plus" youth group at St John's. After three or four years I discovered that there was little chance of becoming a surveyor at Eastwood's so I began applying for other jobs.

Eventually I got a job as a Building Surveying Assistant with the Greater London Council, working in the local branch of their Architects' Department at Greenwich. The office later moved to Rangers House, a beautiful Georgian building in Chesterfield Walk, backing onto Greenwich Park and facing Blackheath. This was a lovely place to work in, overlooking the flowerbeds, the oak, chestnut, and many other trees in the park where Queen Elizabeth I had grown up. In the park there used to be a very ancient oak tree where it is said she used to hide. There were also the remains of an alabaster bath sunk in the ground, which was presumably part of an old palace. Quite near to the Royal Observatory in the park is a splendid bronze statue of General Wolfe as he stands over looking the Royal Naval College and the Queens House below with the Thames flowing behind. As a child I spent many happy times in Greenwich Park with my parents. It was also quite close to home so I would sometimes actually walk to work! One year during the Christmas party I asked permission from my boss to speak to my colleagues about how I became a Christian. I was the youngest person in the office and they were all very friendly. In all about thirty people worked in Rangers House and the surveyors were very helpful giving me technical advice and books. It was like a big family, and sometimes I would go to visit them when they were off sick. During this time Ann and I were married at St John's Blackheath, and we both continued to be very much involved in the youth work at St John's Church. Some two years later I was transferred to the main Architects Department office at County Hall, off the end of Westminster Bridge. Here again the surveyors and architects in our two offices were always ready to advise and help and I soon got promoted.

Chapter 2
PREPARATION AND DEPARTURE

When Dr Livingstone made his cynical remarks about my father's health, I still needed to find out exactly how ill my father was, so I made an appointment to see a senior surgeon at St James Hospital, Balham, where my dad had been operated on. The consultant who had performed the operation was not there, but Mr Swinnerton who had been on the original team was. He was most helpful and said, 'Your father's operation was fully successful; all the cancer was removed and quite a lot more. He is in his sixties, and will not get any younger, but we are confident he is cured. So go ahead with your plans for South America!' I was very reassured and relieved but still felt extremely unsettled.

When the news broke that we were going to Chile there were different reactions from people who knew me. A member of the family, an only child like myself, was concerned when he and his wife heard that we were anticipating going to South America. The wife wrote saying that in no way should we go – my duty was to stay near my parents. Some neighbours, who had known me for many years, felt the same way and it became difficult to talk to them from that time onwards. Another person asked if we would be taking our nine months old son with us (this question puzzled me) and I eventually said 'Well we've never thought of leaving him behind!'

My colleagues at work thought we were very brave when I explained that Ann and I were going out to South America to do reconstruction work after an earthquake. They asked lots of questions and decided to give me a large technical volume called 'Specification', and one of the architects bought me a book on reinforced concrete calculations and design. John continued to write for some time after we arrived in Chile, and went to a great deal of trouble sending me sheets of calculations for a new concrete water tower. As the time drew nearer I found it more and more difficult to concentrate in the office. It seemed as if a great black cloud was hovering over me. To cope with my work I would book in on arrival at the office and then almost immediately book out on site taking all my specifications, drawings, and notebooks with me. At this time colleagues in the Architect's Office at County Hall were very understanding. I always told them where I could be found on site, and they would sort things out or take phone calls and leave messages for me.

I first handed in my notice at the Greater London Council about three months before we were due to sail, but I felt under pressure all the time so withdrew my notice. After this I went back again to see Canon Harry Sutton, the SAMS General Secretary. He said, 'I know both of you find it difficult to make decisions, but if you don't go now you may never go at all!'

Returning to the office I handed my notice in for the second time! When I was summoned to see the Personnel Officer he was very considerate. They had just upgraded me and given me a raise in salary. "Why leave? Could we not offer you some more money?" he asked. I explained that I was very grateful for the offer of yet another increase in salary, but my future income would be a lot less than half what I was earning at present! Eventually he said, 'Well, we shall be sorry to lose you, but be assured if things don't work out there will always be a job here for you!'

Our 'Valedictory'– the old fashioned word for farewell – was held in a hall in central London. Amongst the friends from St John's Blackheath who came was Miss Cole, a retired CMS missionary who was in her eighties and promised to pray regularly for us. Of course they included our Vicar Rev Martin Parsons, and his wife Emily, Len and Edith Bennett, John Hollingsworth and others whose names I have to say I sadly cannot remember now.

Looking at the people in this crowded hall, I now began to realise that we were becoming part of a large extended family called SAMS (the South American Mission Society). This family still continues to grow today and includes people from all over the world. As we stood at the back, waiting to sit down a couple pushed through the crowd to speak to us, they were Colin and Barbara Bazley. Colin immediately took hold of my arm and grabbing my hand said, 'Brother I am so sorry to hear about your dad's illness: we have been praying for you!' I had never met Colin before and yet I suddenly became conscious that here was a brother from Liverpool – a place I had never visited - who was genuinely concerned for me.

As the meeting proceeded, the candidates, who were standing on the platform, were asked to say a few words. Just before that, Major Batt, who was Chairman of the Society, announced that he was extremely sorry that the Jacklins were not able to come due to family illness. Ann and I were sitting near the front of the meeting and I suddenly felt a great surge of adrenalin, really wanting a chance to explain that my father was recovering from major surgery. I felt so angry for it seemed to me that the impression being given was that this "family illness" my dad had was probably flu or something! I felt so hurt, but Ann urged me to remain in my seat and not to embarrass anyone, so I kept quiet.

I finally packed up work on Thursday afternoon and rushed home to spend three days frantically packing. Ann said we would never make it in time, and I must confess that in my heart I felt she might be right! As it happened we didn't have much furniture in our small flat, so after we had given Ann's piano away we were left with our double bed, a dressing table, a tall boy and two or three dining-room chairs. The bed and furniture went to my mother's house and the chairs, with some boxes, to my Aunt Edie.

We finally sailed one very foggy Monday autumn morning in 1962. I had not dared to go to bed the night before fearing I would not wake up in time, so had just over an hour's sleep on my mother's living-room floor. My cousin Bernard had kindly offered to drive us up to Euston, on his way to work, to catch the boat train to Liverpool. Unfortunately it was a really thick pea-souper of a fog in London, added to which my cousin had only just passed his driving test. Ann's dad came with us and was convinced we would miss the train as we continued to get more and more delayed. Arriving at the station we were still afraid we would miss the train, so with our Silver Cross pram with baby Peter inside and a suitcase balanced on top, we began to run non-stop until we found the platform. Fortunately we had not missed the train! However, it was ready to go. A few friends were there, although sadly some had given up on us and had already gone home, so after some very short farewells we climbed on board. In the compartment in the rack above our heads we discovered one or two large packages put on board, which were to travel in our name. At Liverpool docks we quickly embarked on the Reina del Mar, one of the P and O passenger ships. We discovered there were seven of us in all, Colin and Barbara Bazley with baby Katherine, Brian and Gill Skinner, Jean Porter and ourselves with nine-months-old Peter. Our party consisted of a clergyman and his wife, a farmer and his wife, a nurse, and a builder and his wife.

At Liverpool everyone except us seemed to have lots of people at the dockside to see them off, so we were very grateful to the Rev Albert Ormiston who came to bid us farewell on behalf of the mission society. We also felt a bit sorry for ourselves as some members of our party had enormous amounts of flowers filling their cabins from their supporters. The fog, however, had followed us and was so thick in Liverpool it was impossible see the Liver Building. Worse still, within a few minutes of sailing we couldn't see anyone on the dockside either!

Our seven thousand mile journey was to take four weeks, which gave plenty of time to relax, take part in deck games, use the swimming pool, and work through our 'Teach Yourself Spanish' books! Our orders had been to study Spanish during the few weeks that led up to our departure, and I had borrowed a Linguaphone course from the library. However, life was so hectic that we never had time to use it!

Chapter 3
JOURNEY TO SOUTH AMERICA

When we sailed to Chile from Liverpool at the beginning of October on that very foggy day in 1962, our first stop was in France at La Rochelle. Here we walked along the dockside and the French people thought it was extraordinary to see a priest in a clerical collar carrying a little girl on his shoulders. Colin was of course carrying his daughter Katherine who was about a year old. Crossing the Bay of Biscay we stopped at Santander, and walked under the trees with Peter and Katherine in our pram overlooking the vast natural harbour. Around the corner on the Atlantic coast we bought our first Spanish guitar in Vigo. I think it was here that I was fascinated to see the Spanish housewives elegantly carrying dustbins on their heads as they walked up the steep cobbled streets. However, I must surely have offended them because they soon expressed their disapproval when I attempted to photograph them! Our last stop before crossing the Atlantic was Lisbon where I was very impressed by the small single-decker trams. Then for six days we went without seeing land, and passed the Azores at some time during the early hours.

During the journey we met up with Alex Hughes, an officer in the Salvation Army. Alex was in first class and we were in cabin class, but we used to meet up on deck and for prayer meetings. At these meetings there were folk from different nationalities, and some prayed in English, Spanish, German, or whatever language they were used to. It's remarkable to me that you could get the gist of what they were saying without knowing the language, and to be able to say amen! Having crossed the Atlantic we began stopping at various ports on the north coast of South America including Trinidad, La Guaira, Curacao, Cartagena, and Colón.

Although the Reina del Mar was a passenger ship, she carried quite a lot of cargo and so loaded or unloaded goods at most of the ports. This meant we would sometimes stay in port for several hours or even a day or two enabling the passengers to go on shore to look around. One of our first stops was Trinidad, followed by Guaria, Curacao and Cartagena. At the back of town in one of these ports was a market where the indigenous people rented some workshops. Here they made pottery, leather and wooden goods, and we bought some finely carved Indian figures and a very life like bust of Cervantes, the writer of Don Quixote, which people say now looks like me with my beard! I still can't believe this beautifully carved life-like bust only cost me five dollars! In Colombia as we looked down from the ship to the dockside, crowds of small boys fascinated us by diving below the water to retrieve coins or oranges, thrown to them from the ship's dining room.

We spent a few hours in Colón, the last stop before the Panama Canal, and found clothes and electrical goods extremely cheap. The next day we were taken by surprise when we suddenly realised we were passing through the canal just before breakfast. It was a fantastic experience watching the powerful little donkey engines chugging along the rails on both sides of the ship as we were towed through the many locks! I think it must have taken at least a whole day moving slowly through the canal and tree lined lakes, passing undergrowth and steaming jungle. Once through the canal we soon travelled down the Pacific coast of South America stopping at Callao, which allowed us to have a few hours in Lima. As Peru's capital is near the port we decided to get a taxi to the city's museum. The journey only took about 40 minutes, and we were very impressed with the politeness of the driver. Until, that is, he drove us back to the port in ten minutes and we realised we had been literally taken for a ride! At one of these ports there were large numbers of pelicans perched everywhere, especially on the tops of the lamp standards along the dockside. Looking up to the surrounding cliffs we could see pelican droppings covering the tops to a thickness of several feet. This "abono" is used as a natural fertilizer and is one of the country's most lucrative exports!

Soon continuing to move south, we had our first glimpse of Chile at Arica, where the ship had to stand out from the shore because the water was so shallow. I understand this has now all changed and Arica has its own very modern harbour. Next came Antofagasta, and finally Valparaiso, Chile's most important commercial and naval port. At some stage going through customs we looked across the customs hall to see that Alex Hughes was having difficulties. The customs officials were holding up large quantities of ladies' underwear that he had in his luggage, and as Alex was single they wanted to know what it was all for. Senior officers from the Salvation Army were summoned to assist Alex and they managed to explain to the customs men that the underwear was actually needed by the lady officers in Chile. Alex had been requested to bring this in his luggage from England as such items were unavailable in Chile, so finally the customs men let him go through!

Arrival and Welcome

At Valparaiso the Rev David Pytches (as he was then) was waiting for us on the dockside. He soon whisked us all home and surprisingly ushered us into the church hall! Here David had used his practical skills to create a family flat for Mary and the children at the back under the balcony of the church hall. We soon discovered that we would also enjoy the benefits of David's innovative work, as he had built several guest bedrooms at the other end of the hall. As someone said 'we never realised that to be missionaries meant going on the stage!' During the next week or so we went down to the docks each day to see our luggage through customs. Afterwards David then arranged for a lorry to transport all our stuff down to the south.

We then all travelled by train to Santiago and changed onto the overnight corridor train to Temuco. We were so impressed to see the magnificent leather seats with bunks over, complete with crisp white sheets.

Early in the morning there was knock on the door and the steward asked if we would like a cup of tea. We rather confused the poor man by saying 'Yes, but could we have milk in our tea please?' Some time later to our great amazement, Ann and I were handed two cups of steaming hot milk with tea bags in! We had inadvertently discovered that South Americans never take milk in their tea! However, we were later served with an excellent cooked breakfast of scrambled eggs, bacon, and buttered toast in our compartment. Almost immediately after breakfast we arrived at Temuco railway station, and were met by on the platform by a crowd of people, including senior English and American missionaries. Some of the Americans were from the "Strong's Mission", which had started working amongst Chilean army personnel, and had then gone on to start several Churches which they called Centros Biblicos (Bible Centres). Their director, Bill Strong, and his wife continued to be very kind to us, later lending us a vehicle to enable us to go on our first holiday. Arriving at the Temuco Centre it was decided that Colin and Barbara should go straight to Chol Chol, and the rest of us, including Jean Porter, Brian and Gill Skinner, plus ourselves would go to Maquehue Pelal to the Mission farm. I came to realise that seven new missionaries all arriving at once had created a bit of an accommodation crisis and they didn't really know where to put us all! It was then that I came to recall the words of Canon Harry Sutton who had said, 'You may have to start off by building your own house!' But fortunately it never came to that!

Chapter 4
MAQUEHUE PELAL AND THE FARM

Kathleen Clark was running the farm when we arrived, awaiting the arrival of Brian Skinner, the new Farm Manager. The farm, located some eighteen miles from Temuco, also provided land on which was built the hospital, church and local school. Kathleen had been doing a great job because by training and experience she was an R.E. Teacher. As we were dropped off at the farmhouse Kathleen came out to welcome us, and I shall never forget meeting her on that very wet autumn afternoon. Her heavy trench coat was soaked and her brown suede shoes were oozing with water, but she gave us such a broad smile that we immediately felt at home. We then lived in the farmhouse for our next year, with Ann and Kathleen sharing the housekeeping.

Officially we were to be given no formal language study by other missionaries as it was considered that this might cause us to pick up all their bad accents and grammatical mistakes! After a short period I became so thoroughly frustrated with this policy that I decided to try to attend evening classes at the North American Institute in Temuco. Yet to get there was almost impossible. There was only one bus a day and the bus stop was over a mile away. One possible alternative was to walk or cycle for an hour and a half to Quepe railway station and take a regional bus along the Pan American Highway to Temuco. The better alternative was a shorter distance walking across beautiful countryside, along footpaths through woods and fields, but this was just too muddy in the winter! In theory, of course, cycling along the longer route should have been quickest. However, we are talking here of an earth road full of great potholes and large stones that bounced and sped through the air when the occasional vehicle drove past, which also enveloped you in clouds of choking dust in the summer as everything was so dry.

The other important factor was that the bicycle was extremely old and battered! Apart from the saddle giving you a very painful ride, bits frequently fell off or the bike broke down leaving you completely stranded! So I had little choice but to get used to walking the hour and a half's journey on foot to the main Pan American Highway! From here I could usually get a bus to Temuco.

Winter mornings in southern Chile were very cold, crisp and beautiful as I walked back home. The hoar frost created intricate patterns on the long grasses and wire fences and the many water filled potholes in the road would often turn to solid ice! On the other hand, nearly without fail each afternoon around two o'clock the sun would come out and its welcome rays made things considerably warmer outside the house than in. I loved to look across the landscape towards the Andes where volcano Villarrica snuggled amongst the mountains. This old white-capped giant would always have a faint horizontal wisp of white smoke that contrasted with the blue cloudless sky. It seemed as if he were saying 'You may think I am asleep, but I'm not really!' The Chilean flag is red, white and blue, where I am told the blue represents the sky, the white the snow of the Andes, and the red the blood of the Indian people slaughtered in their thousands by the Spanish conquerors!

During our time in Maquehue the Bible Institute was held in the farmhouse in the winter months, and Kathleen would usually prepare her classes outside on the balcony in the warm afternoon sunshine. The kitchen was the only room in the farmhouse that had heating; there the wood burning stove provided hot water and was used for cooking. Old Don Carmelo, who had been nursed by Helen Bridge through a very serious illness, used to chop the wood, keep the fire going in the kitchen and look after the horses. He would always keep a teapot on the hob and would re-use the tealeaves over and over again, even drying out the tea bags on the stove. A cup of tea therefore tended to be just a warm colourless liquid! One day Ann and I were going into Temuco shopping and decided to leave a large bunch of grapes on the kitchen table, telling Don Carmelo to help himself. Returning late that afternoon we searched for the grapes, and eventually had to ask where they were? He replied; 'Well, you did say help yourself'; so we discovered he had eaten the lot all two kilos! Why not? After all grapes grow in abundance in Chile and are very cheap to buy. Our sharp learning curve had started and we were beginning to learn something about the culture!

Chilean Generosity

We were soon to appreciate that Chilean people are extremely generous, always giving you small presents and especially fruit, so over the years we have learnt to do the same! One day I had gone to Temuco to buy some nails, and getting off the bus realised I didn't have enough money. Seeing someone I knew very well, I asked if he could lend me some cash. He apologised and said he didn't have any! Finding this strange I asked how that was. So he replied, 'Well, a friend of mine's shoes were worn out and he needed some new ones, so I gave him my last twenty pounds!' 'Did you lend him the money?' I asked. 'Of course not,' he answered 'he needed the money and I didn't, so I gave it to him!'

Peter had his first birthday at the farmhouse, and the local headmaster's wife brought him a present. She came with something covered with a clean tea towel, and suddenly to our great surprise removed the cloth to reveal a live hen! 'It would provide fresh eggs for the little boy' she explained! So wonderful and generous! I wonder how many of us would have thought of that.

Peter's first birthday party 1963. Outside the farmhouse, Maquehue Pelal, Chile

During that first year we did have one serious scare when Peter started to walk and we thought we had lost him! We were horrified and after making frantic enquiries we were told by the cowman, Don Domingo, that he had seen the little lad heading off down towards the river! Fortunately he hadn't got very far and Pedro, one of the other farm workers, brought him back to the house! The main problem was that there were at least four doors leading out of the farmhouse, and the country people tended to come in and out without shutting them!

Life on the Farm

The farm always assisted the local Indian farmers and loaned out pairs of oxen for ploughing and heavy tasks. The sale of the farm's wheat harvest was paid into an account and mainly used to supplement the poorer pastors with a living allowance. Many of the Mapuches were poor by our standards but most had their own plots of land. The farm had several horses, which were used mainly for visiting the small country churches on Sundays and also by the Bible Institute students.

Across the river beyond the church was a timber house called Aluhuen built by Charles Sadleir a Canadian missionary who came to Chile in the early part of the twentieth century. In the front garden was a beautiful maple tree that he had brought from Canada. Its magnificent branches were covered with red, yellow and brown leaves of varying shades during autumn. In the house Charles had met with Mapuche chiefs to translate the Bible and Hymn Book into their mother tongue, and installed his own printing press for the purpose. He had previously worked before ordination in gaining land rights for the Canadian Indians. He was therefore very qualified to work amongst the Mapuches Indians and was highly esteemed by them. Later because of his great commitment to them they made him an honorary chief.

We had been in Maquehue for just on three months when Kathleen asked Ann if she would like to cook the food for the men harvesting the wheat. They were actually contractors who came each year with their machines, moving from one farm to another in the area. I thought Ann had done really well in making soups, stews and bread on a wood-burning stove, with no fresh water on tap, and no shops nearby, until one evening I realised it seemed rather dark on the back balcony. A crowd of workman had cast an ominous shadow across the windows. We soon discovered we had a strike on our hands. 'The Señora doesn't give us enough meat' they complained. 'Usually the farm kills two sheep a day to feed the harvesters!' We had no idea that this was so and after a quick conversation with Brian Skinner, the new Farm Manager, this was rectified the following day and the men called off the strike! It was decided to pay a local lady in the future to do the cooking as she was much more accustomed to the way the men liked their food! The men worked like Trojans from sunrise to sun set for five or six days until the harvest was all in. They slept in the open air each night under the machines and bullock carts so they could guard the sacks of grain from being stolen during the night. It was also very heavy work – so I discovered when I offered to help carry some sacks of wheat to the barn. Getting the sack on my back, I then collapsed with the eighty kilos weight pinning me to the ground! I still have great admiration for the farm men as they were always covered with all the dust and dirt that came with unloading and loading these extremely heavy sacks of wheat into the grain store.

Poor local families, knowing a new family had arrived in the area, hoped we needed assistance to help in the house with cooking, washing and cleaning. We found this whole idea of having a maid quite unacceptable and extremely embarrassing! Later, however, we came to learn that many young women needed the work, and after working for a little while for a missionary family they could get a good reference enabling them to get a job with a middle class Chilean family.

Riding on the Top Deck!

A couple of interesting incidents happened to me during my first year of attempts at language study. I would start out from the farmhouse in the early afternoon. Occasionally instead of walking I would go by bicycle and leave it at the house of our Pastor's sister, opposite the bus stop near the main road. Arriving one day I could see people already standing at the stop as the bus was due any moment.

Quickly running across the road as the bus arrived, I indicated to the driver that I wanted to put the bicycle on the roof. It was normal practice for the country people to carry things on the bus roof. Everything went on the roof including sacks of wheat, flour, potatoes, cement, mattresses, crates of live chickens, sheep, and even pigs! Indeed the latter would sometimes urinate down the windows when they were scared! So this day, hoisting the bicycle onto my shoulder I climbed up the ladder and walked along the roof to put it down. That was O.K. until suddenly, without warning; the bus lurched forward and was off speeding down the road – with me standing on the roof! Scared stiff I threw myself down onto the roof, and realising the bus wasn't going to stop, began hammering on the roof with my fists shouting at the top of my voice! The bus eventually did stop and I was able to climb down, feeling very shaken. On entering the bus I paid the driver my fare, walked to the back and sat down with great relief. Then, almost as if they had practised it, the whole busload of people turned their heads to have a look at this 'mad gringo! 'Gringo' by the way is just another word for foreigner, usually a blonde-haired white skinned English speaking person. A Chilean friend said, "The word 'Gringo' could mean you're a bit confused and don't understand." I can identify with that!

Going Under – Then Saved

The second incident was even more life threatening. I had decided to leave the farmhouse earlier and walk to the Pan American Highway this afternoon. It was wintertime and as it got dark earlier I decided to take a short cut across country. Getting to where the small bridge was, which was just a heavy plank, to my horror I found it was missing! Frantically walking up and down I began to search for a place where the water was shallow. At last I found a small waterfall where the water was only a few inches deep. I was so worried about missing the bus I decided I must risk walking across. Placing my Spanish books under my arm and carrying my heavy commando shoes in one hand I stepped into the water. I had noticed a certain amount of green weed under the water, but I began to walk gingerly along the rock edge. I was feeling quite relieved and gave a deep sigh as I had almost reached the other bank. Then suddenly I lost my footing on the slippery surface and plunged into the water.

I must have gone down about three metres before coming up again. I managed to hurl my shoes towards the bank, before going down again. I was wearing a heavy tweed jacket and my nylon raincoat had somehow filled up with air underneath. I was not scared at first, but then started to, think 'You're only supposed to go down three times before you drown!' Just before going down the next time I thought heard a noise behind me, and cranking my neck round could see someone standing on the rock ledge with a hand outstretched towards me. I grabbed the hand and the man pulled me out of the water. Then beckoning to me to follow he led me up the bank to his 'ruca'. That is the traditional single-storey house with straw walls and a thatched roof used by the Mapuche Indians.

Our conversation was very limited but he demonstrated great kindness and generosity, as I tried to understand what he was saying to me. As I watched he moved behind a cloth curtain made of flour sacks and emerged with a blue serge suit on a hanger. This was obviously his best and only suit and indicating with his index finger he offered it to me to wear. The only other trousers he had were the jeans he was wearing. Next I understood him to be speaking about a horse – and I eventually realised he was offering to lend me his horse! Finally I discovered he was apologising because he hoped I could ride without a saddle, because he was too poor to own a saddle! The cost, I later discovered, was about equal to the price of a horse! In the country Chilean children often ride bareback quite expertly. Now I began to shake my head however; in no way could I ride his horse without a saddle. I'd only had three very basic riding lessons just before leaving England. So saying 'gracias' several times I began my long walk back to the farm, and as it was almost dark so I needed to get a move on!

Nearing home, after passing through a wood, I began to approach the house of Don Herminio the Pastor, just a little way from the church. Walking along the earth road I began to hear the dogs barking on the other side of the hedge. It was now pitch black and I suddenly sensed that several snarling dogs were all around me – pinning me back into the hedge. However I later began to feel that possibly they were as scared of me as I was of them! After what seemed a very long time fortunately the door to the house opened and a beam of light shone out, Maria the Pastor's wife called the dogs off and then shut the door again! She never seemed to give a thought as to who might be causing the commotion. When I arrived at the Farm House it was around eight in the evening. Ann was sitting in the dining room – and was very surprised to see me. Not seeming to notice my hair was soaking wet she greeted me by saying 'Why haven't you gone to your class, and where did you get that suit from? I can't remember what I was wearing on my feet – I was probably bare foot – for I had already lost one of my heavy Commando shoes before being pulled out of the water!

Spiritual Turmoil

This was the last time I would go to my Spanish class from the farm. It was all too difficult and I began to get very depressed and really fed up with God. I began feeling very angry, thinking this whole venture was a complete waste of time! How would I ever speak Spanish and communicate with the workmen on the building sites? How can you supervise building work when you can't speak the language? I began to feel it was all a big mistake and I should never have come to Chile!

Kathleen, however, was very patient with me and gave me a little booklet by George Duncan called 'The Dark night of the Soul'. Also at about this time, or soon after, I wrote asking my father to send me a book called 'Spiritual Depression' (based on the Psalms) by Dr Martin Lloyd-Jones. Seeing this book in the dining room someone commented 'Oh you need to read that before getting depressed!' They had no idea of the great spiritual and mental turmoil I had been going through!

Some days later Kathleen suggested I might like to go with her to return the clothes the man had lent me and she would thank him for his great kindness. We used two of the farm's horses, which of course had saddles! When Kathleen met the man he explained that he realised that I must have come from the Mission farm, and because of its good name he wanted to help me in any way he could. The explanation for the missing plank was that someone must have taken it for firewood!

Language Tales
Sometimes on a Saturday afternoon Ann, Peter and I would go out for a walk and visit one of the local people. Everyone was extremely kind and always welcomed visitors. On one of these afternoons Don Herminio and his wife María invited us over to see them. As we arrived María was making 'Sopaipillas' in a large pan of boiling oil. These are really small doughnuts cooked in boiling oil, sweet-flavoured and eaten hot. It was a great afternoon spent sipping many cups of tea and consuming lots of hot sopaipillas, until finally we decided we ought to return to the farmhouse. With my very limited Spanish I think I said something like "Thank you for this afternoon, we now ought to go home for tea!" I still feel embarrassed when I think about this faux pas! (How can you say you must go home for tea when you've been having tea and cakes all the afternoon?)
Later I came to learn that Chilean people have lots of anecdotes about missionaries struggling with the language. A single female nurse returned after visiting a sick patient, calling Don Carmelo over she asked him to take the reins and steady the horse as she dismounted. What she actually said was 'I'm about to get down, would you take my clothes off now, please?' Knowing Don Carmelo I don't think he batted an eyelid! During our time at the farmhouse Kathleen was also in charge of the Bible Institute with the Rev Herminio Merino, Pastor of the church at Maquehue, sharing the teaching with her.

Rats!

The female students slept above our bedroom, up a wooden staircase in the roof space. One problem was that there were a large number of rats living in the house as well. In the middle of most nights there would be quite a lot of activity going on with rats coming down these stairs dragging saucers of rat poison with them! The sort of noise we would hear would be bonk, scrape, scrape, and then bonk again! The rats were so hungry they used to chew all the edges of the plastic plates when the poison was finished. Unfortunately one night Zoila Pranao, one of the girls, had a large part of her long woollen coat eaten, and had to cut several inches off the bottom and make a new hem! Zoila became a very good friend of ours and later went on to become a nurse in Santiago.

At the farm all the lights went out at 9.00 pm as this was when the generator at the water mill stopped working. Of course when the nurses had an emergency, or had to deliver a baby during the night, the generator was set in motion again. Light switches were never turned off, so the lights automatically came on whenever the generator began working. I had decided to make a connecting doorway between our bedroom and the small room next door where Peter slept. Strangely not long after he would frequently wake up in the night and cry. There seemed to be no apparent reason for this, until as we looked more carefully we saw rat droppings all around the edge of his blanket! One night we were unexpectedly awakened to find all the lights on at 3.00 am.

Then suddenly to my horror I saw a big black shiny rat eating a bar of chocolate on our dressing table, a special present brought out from England for Ann by Harry Sutton! Feeling I must do something I quickly leapt out of bed, and then had such a fright as the creature ran across my bare feet to make his exit. Subsequently in my confusion I slipped up on the carpet, my feet shot in the air and with a great vibrating thud I landed flat on my back on the polished floor!

Rats really enjoyed getting into the cellar under the kitchen floor where the apples were stored. Sometimes there was a suspicious sweet aroma almost like cider wafting up from the cellar, giving away the fact that the rats had been feasting on the apples! There was an absolute army of them at the farm, many coming from the barns at the back of the house where the grain was stored. One morning, seeing a large fat rat sitting on some wooden steps I thought I would be really brave. I was sure he was probably suffering from the effects of rat poison so was rather groggy and not going to run away quickly. Creeping forward I raised the shovel I was carrying to give him such a mighty swipe, but unfortunately I missed and brought it down with a tremendous bang on the steps. The rat was quite unconcerned and just popped under the barn steps and silently slipped away, whereas I had to suffer from a sprained wrist for weeks! During winter months the weather was so cold in the house that we usually went to bed early. In the bedrooms it was literally freezing so most nights we just gathered up all the woven carpets and put them on the bed as extra covers! Admittedly, this made it warmer, yet very difficult to turn over or sit up but well worth it!

Carpentry Classes

After some time I began to wonder why we had to be stuck out on a farm in the middle of rural Chile? The farm needed no new building for me to construct, and there was certainly not a lot else to do! Though to be fair, on the farm there was living accommodation where we could stay, as there was nowhere else to live! Kathleen had obviously been praying about this so one day she asked me if I would like to take the Bible Institute students for carpentry in the afternoons. They only had classes in the mornings, so in the afternoons they took part in practical things like working in the kitchen garden or doing repairs to the farm buildings. A disused store at the back of the farmhouse was made available with Brian Skinner's permission and we converted this into a carpentry workshop. Máximo Cheuquelaf was appointed as my deputy as he had been taught to make furniture in the Methodist Industrial School. We soon became good friends, and he was extremely patient with me, as I still couldn't speak Spanish.

At the end of each afternoon we would look at our watches and then begin to clear up and put the tools away. The most embarrassing thing for me was that at this point Maximo would always say 'Qué mas?' But I could never understand what that meant, and would ask him to repeat it! Eventually I came to understand that all he was saying "Is there anything else to do?" At times I would hold up a tool to see if the students could tell me what it was called in Spanish. The reply would often be that they didn't know a word for that because they were farmers. Over the months Maximo and I, the students, were able to make a number of things like communion tables, lecterns and simple pews for use in the country churches.

The Mapuches

Later Kathleen discussed with Pastor Herminio the idea of asking me to build a church at a place called Laurel Huacho. The land there belonged to the Torres family and one of their sons had died of tuberculosis. He had become a Christian due to the loving care he received in the Maquehue Hospital, and the family were so grateful that they wanted to dedicate the church to his memory. Sadly during our early years in Chile nearly every Mapuche family had at least one member suffering from active tuberculosis. The hospital at Maquehue had a capacity of thirty beds, and was founded by Christian nurses mainly for the treatment of this disease. The hospital was very highly regarded in this region of Southern Chile because of the great care and immense dedication of the nurses and staff. Some time later when I was able to understand Spanish Maximo told me that several close members of his family had died from tuberculosis.

The Mapuche traditional religion is animism, a belief that trees, inanimate objects and natural phenomena all have a soul. They also accept the idea of a supernatural power. The people often have a fear of attack by evil spirits, and Christian leaders are sometimes called in to cast out these spirits. The witch doctors are always women called Machis who have their own cures and some effective herbal remedies. The march of progress has now reached Chol Chol and we have been told that the Machi now actually has her own surgery. Patients have to speak to the receptionist to get an appointment these days!

During the Spanish conquest in the sixteenth century the Mapuche were fierce fearless fighters. Copying the Spaniards they soon mastered the use of horses in battle and were never subjugated. They still continue to be a proud, dignified and intelligent people. Some sources say that there are 400,000 Mapuches living in Chile today. During the 1930's the SAMS had helped to establish between thirty and forty rural schools in the south. Some of these schoolhouses went on to be used as churches as well. Both William Wilson and Dorothy Royce were awarded gold medals by the Chilean government for their work in education and medicine. SAMS has always been at the forefront of medical and educational work, especially in the rural areas in the south where there was a great shortage of schools and medical work.

Fiestas

During the summer the local country churches around Maquehue Pelal had their annual festival of 'Alabanzas', or praises. These were usually held on public holidays or weekends when people would come from different areas dressed in their traditional clothes. The ladies wore their black dresses and colourful shawls, with silver necklaces and head-dresses adorned with silver coins Some of the men dressed in dark narrow trousers with a red woven sashes in place of a belt together with a waistcoat and small colourful silk poncho. Their heavy silver spurs could be as large as saucers, and if they could afford it some would wear knee-length riding boots of beautifully sculptured leather. Their stirrups were made of wood, similar to ornately carved clogs, and were better than metal stirrups as your feet did not accidentally slip out of them! Hats were mainly of the wide-brimmed felt type, or straw ones like those used for working in the fields. Some families came to these festivals on foot, but others who had elderly grandparents or children would travel by ox cart. In their homes many of the women would have large wooden looms upon which they would weave woollen '*mantas*' (ponchos), colourful carpets, cushion covers and other articles all woven with traditional or Indian designs.

During festival meal times families would light small open fires to boil kettles for maté tea, and sit around in groups. The trees offered shade and small wisps of smoke from the fires could be seen curling up through the branches, whilst the horses waited patiently nearby. Sometimes these Christian festivals would include baptisms by immersion in the local river, and if the bishop was present candidates were confirmed close by in the open air.

At other times groups of men from other communities gathered near the school football pitch to take part in all day football tournaments. Here the winning team would not be presented with a cup or shield, but a couple of sheep quietly standing tethered to a tree until the end of the competition.

When the local school children realised there was a new family living at the farmhouse, they would pick blackberries in the hedgerows and sell them to us. Alternatively they would barter these or other things for second-hand clothes. The country people hardly ever troubled to pick blackberries for themselves because they rarely ate stewed fruit, and would never make puddings or jam. Local schoolboys loved to catch small rainbow trout in the river and would bring these up to the farmhouse hoping we would buy them.

Over the River Quepe

A few hundred yards from the farmhouse stands the suspension bridge spanning the river Quepe. It reminded me of some of Brunel's suspension bridges, which were of course built of steel. The bridge across the Quepe was constructed with stout timber towers at each end, with thick wire cables suspended across to support the long timber beams made of eucalyptus. These beams were covered transversely with thick wooden planks, with gaps in between through which you could see the river way below, making it a bit scary as you walked across. The bridge would snake up and down and sway from side to side if a lorry drove across. It was used mainly by oxcarts or for getting cattle across the river. Apart from vertical rods it had no sides and occasionally animals did fall off. I remember a young steer falling off and being later found wandering in the shallows below the bridge. Unfortunately it had lost an eye but seemed to have no other serious injuries!

It was extremely helpful to have the hospital just across the river so that we could pop in if a child or one of us was unwell. It had no doctor but the nurses could usually sort us out. It was just a short walk across the bridge, along a pathway across a field with the orchard and hospital on the left, and the timber built church on the right. During our first year we worshipped there and remember some services being in total darkness when the belt broke on the generator at the farm's water mill. We were always conscious of a strange, strong smell in Church. It turned out to be caused by bats nesting in the roof. Obviously we had not noticed their droppings on the seats, as we had never seen this sort of thing before! Some evenings in church, when the lights went out, one of the nurses would bring a paraffin lamp over from the hospital. The services being in Spanish meant I didn't get much out of them, but I was fascinated because Pastor Herminio would lead singing and actually preach in the pitch dark! Most people in England complain about church services, but at least this was different! You didn't even have to look at the Vicar!

Tracking the Route to Laurel Huacho

One Sunday morning it was agreed that I cycle to Laurel Huacho with Don Herminio. It was a very hot summer's day as we set off with him in front and me following as he knew the way! Of course, the bike was still the old one borrowed from the farm, and we had been riding for about an hour. Suddenly my handlebars fell off and I was frantically fighting to get them back on again! Looking up for assistance, I found that Herminio had not waited for me and, to my horror, was already out of sight! I began to feel sick and desperate! Here I was all on my own in the middle of South America, not knowing where I was, not being able to speak the language, and with no one to ask anyway! 'O Lord you've just got to help me!' I shouted aloud. Eventually I did get the handlebars back on again, but I then said to myself, 'Where do I go from here?' Then looking down at the earth road I thought, 'Surely a Boy Scout would follow Herminio's tyre tracks?' Actually that was not too difficult as there were no other tracks in the dust at that time in the morning! So I was encouraged until later I found I had lost the tracks – they had vanished altogether! Again I began to experience moments of great panic! After a few more minutes of absolute desperation I again managed to pull myself together! Searching around carefully I found the tracks had suddenly turned left across a field, and then veered to the left of two tall laurel trees. Behind the trees was the Torres' house. And to my great relief I could see Herminio sitting in the open doorway sipping a cool drink! Even now I still have a nagging feeling that he was grinning at me! I had arrived at Laurel Huacho!

Assembling and Trembling

The following week I bought most of the struts and rafters from a timber yard in Temuco, and the farm lorry collected it. I could begin to assemble the sections for the prefabricated church. All had to be ready before the end of the summer as the earth roads would be impassable for the farm lorry to get to Laurel Huacho in the winter. Riding though puddles on such earth roads in winter often meant the water came above the horse's belly, making the journey impossible. With this in mind it was imperative that I got on with the work as soon as possible. One morning a short while afterwards I was kneeling down in a field behind the farm buildings, hammering nails into the timber frames. I was conscious of a strange, still silence, no birds seemed to be singing and the farm animals were mysteriously quiet. Then without warning, gradually but distinctly, I began to feel the timber frame moving under me, and soon it was going up and down like a boat in rough water! As I looked up across the landscape I could then see the fields for miles rising and falling like the waves of the sea. Tall trees, telegraph poles, fence posts and anything vertical, including the farm buildings, were all swaying from side to

58

side, just as if some powerful wind were blowing! I was experiencing my first earthquake! Within just a few seconds it was all over, and once again you could hear the sound of the birds and animals around you! One evening a few days later several of us were praying in the dining room when we became aware that the house was moving. Glancing up at the corner of the room you could see the angle stretch open and then squeeze back again, just like the opening and closing of a large pair of scissors! The experience of these first earth tremors began to make me feel far safer in the flexible old timber buildings than in the more rigid concrete and brick ones!

At the end of the summer I was taken with Maximo in the old farm lorry, carrying the sectional timber church to Laurel Huacho. On arrival the first thing that intrigued me was the way the country people quickly dug holes in the ground into which they sank short lengths of tree trunk. These were first charred in an open fire to prevent them rotting, and then upon them were placed the wooden wall plates which would support the sides of the building! Once these were in position we could fix the rafters on top that would support the roof covering. The corrugated roof sheeting would be purchased later and fixed by the church members themselves. The roof was the most expensive part and meant months of sacrificial giving by the church members.

In southern Chile I learnt so much about sacrificial Christian giving. These small farmers would give a tenth of their farm produce to be auctioned and the money then went into a regional pastor's fund. The majority of the pastors received no church salary and worked on their land. The only ones with a regular income would be the few who were country schoolteachers.

Maximo and I stayed for several days in Laurel Huacho sleeping on a large wooden double bed in one of the men's bedrooms, which was actually a separate building. Each morning we longed to get up as the mattress consisted of a large sheepskin laid on boards, with heavy 'mantas' (Ponchos) as covers, with the fleas having a feast of a time! Two of the older daughters gave us a call around 6.00 am and brought buckets of cold water from the river, placing them outside for us to wash in. We had meals with the family and in the evenings enjoyed chicken or pork stew (Cazuela), and homemade bread. After the evening meal the father led us in a time of hymn singing and prayer (in almost complete darkness) and the mother kept us going with maté tea.

Chilean maté is made with a few teaspoonfuls of light-brown coloured tea imported from Argentina. It is brewed in a special open topped ceramic or copper pot, about the size of a teacup, to which lump sugar is added with boiling water poured on top. Sometimes a herb, like mint might be, is added to flavour it. I have also had it made with hot milk but this would be very rare. The Paraguayans also drink maté but that is usually quite bitter, and made with cold water. In Chile a silver straw is inserted into the cup at the beginning, and once the maté is brewed the lady of the house passes the cup to the honoured guest first. After you have had a few sucks you pass the cup back to her, she wipes the silver straw, adds more sugar lumps and tops it up with boiling water (usually from the kettle on the open wood fire on the earth floor). Drinking maté is something the country people really enjoy in the evenings. After a hard day's work in the fields it can be very pleasant to sit around the open fire chatting and sipping maté. Some country folk will not come out into the cold evening air after drinking maté, as they believe this could cause a heart attack! I don't really know if there is any medical evidence for this, or if it's just a bit of superstition!

Before the autumn Bishop Ken Howell came up to Laurel Huacho to dedicate the new building. The people had made it look fantastic with garlands of flowers all around the entrance and flowers inside. After the service of dedication the Torres family provided a multi-course lunch in the open air served on long tables under the shade of the grapevines. The cazuela consisted of pork stew cooked with vegetables, followed by about three large plates of dark brown beans. Once the church building was finished Maximo and I returned to the farm and continued working in the carpentry workshop during the Bible Institute. Most of our time was spent making simple furniture, like lecterns and communion tables for the country churches. Maximo was later ordained and he and his family were moved to Santiago where he had his own church. Years later I visited him there where we had a wonderful meal with his wife and grown-up family and he invited me to preach in his church in the evening.

Eruptions

For our very first holiday in Chile we were allowed to camp by a beautiful lake called Licanray about three miles from volcano Villarrica. As we didn't have a tent we were given permission to use a rustic log cabin on a site used by Bill Strong's Church members for

Lake Licanray – our first holiday site

Volcano Villarrica

Volcano Lliama (in winter), near Temuco

their summer camps. On arrival we were so exhausted we laid out our ground sheets and quickly got into our sleeping bags lying on the sandy floor. Up early the next day we all went bathing at the shallow edge of the lake. It was absolutely idyllic surrounded by hills and mountains with many different shades of blues and browns reflected in the lake. I had never seen water so clean and clear, in fact so transparent that you could see the fish swimming around you as you stood on the sandy bottom. The second night we went to bed early and soon it began to rain, with the drops drumming heavily on the corrugated iron roof. Then came some very loud claps of thunder with flashes of lightning brightening up the sky all around us. The storm went on late into the night. Yet although the rain had stopped the thunder seemed to continue, the claps interspersed with great orange and yellow surges of light filling the sky! In the end I decided I should at least go outside and have a look before going to sleep. As I watched I suddenly began to realise that what we thought was thunder could actually be our old sleeping friend Villarrica erupting! In the end we went to bed having decided there wasn't much we could do about it!

The following morning everything was so incredibly quiet that after breakfast I decided to do a bit of exploring. I began to climb the wooded hill immediately behind us, and after about three quarters of an hour I managed to reach the top. Looking across a wide valley I saw the whole landscape had been burnt by fire. Many trees were just smoking, charred trunks, with the grass and undergrowth burnt black and still smouldering with a haze of smoke hanging over the valley. The volcano was back to normal now with its wisp of white smoke floating horizontally across the blue sky and had returned to being the sleeping giant with which we were more familiar.

At a later date whilst living in Temuco we were awakened one night to watch volcano Llaima erupt after several heavy falls of snow. This time there were columns of black smoke rising from two craters tinged with bright red and blue flames. As the heat melted the snow large black patches appeared on the lower slopes. On this occasion we didn't feel scared for the eruption was a long way off and we could enjoy the spectacle from our own bedroom window, almost as if we were watching a giant Roman candle in a faraway firework display.

Chapter 5
TEMUCO AND OTHER JOBS

With no vehicle available for me it was decided after a year on the farm to move us to Temuco a town with a population of some 120,000. Here I could use coach or train to get me to potential building sites in other parts of the country. In Temuco's main plaza is a statue dedicated to a German engineer called Smidt, just across from the old timber Anglican church standing in the corner. The rebuilding work, which I had been sent out to do following the big earthquake of 1960, was now almost complete. Part of my job also included the design of House Churches in the new housing estates. These houses were to be large enough for a family with a lounge downstairs big enough for meetings. Before we arrived the Chilean government had offered a free site to any denomination that could put a church building on it. Unfortunately soon after the next elections the new government legislated that these sites had to be paid for, and that finished the project!

Our first home in Temuco was a ground floor flat belonging to the church treasurer in a street called Las Heras. Furniture amounted to a round table, three rush dining room chairs, and a glass cabinet, all lent to us by a very generous lay preacher called Antonio Villarroel. We were told that if we wanted a double bed, we had to get one made (and pay for it ourselves) as Chileans didn't have double beds! If we wanted a mattress it needed to be made of sheep's wool and be especially ordered and made to fit the bed! Now, apart from an occasional prayer or staff meeting I had nothing to do, so I spent most of my time struggling with Spanish sitting at our splendid round table in our sparsely furnished flat! I looked forward to the services on Sundays but found it very hard to get much out of them. Sometimes the hymn tunes were familiar but of course the words were all in Spanish. In the 1960's our service book was still the old 1662 Prayer Book in formal Spanish The services still included prayers for King George VI, with additional prayers for the President of the United States, the Chilean President Jorge Alessandri, and the Chilean government.

Struggles
One morning I called in at the Mission Centre by the Church to pick up our mail and stay for a cup of coffee. An English lady in her seventies also popped in and introduced herself. 'I'm Struggles to

most people!' she said quietly. 'I know you are new, what are you doing with yourself?" Good question I thought! 'Well I'm not doing very much, as most of the building work is finished now' I replied. Struggles had a certain twinkle in her eye, and went on to say how for many years she had visited the local prison, but added that she had not been recently. 'Would you like to go – we could go together one day?' she continued. So it was that I began prison visiting for the next three years.

Struggles – her real name was Eleanor Strugnell – was a schoolteacher and had originally gone to Argentina to teach. From there she had visited Chile and later married Canon William Wilson, who had founded the Mission School in Chol Chol. He had died in his nineties by which time he had become totally blind. He had been a medical missionary working tirelessly in the country and had founded the boarding school in Chol Chol, more recently called the William Wilson School. He is still tremendously esteemed by the Mapuche Indians for all the work he did amongst them, and was also honoured by the Chilean government in recognition for all his wonderful work.

Struggles was a remarkable woman being very thin and wiry and such a great challenge and encouragement to all of us younger ones. She lived in a tall timber house on the outskirts of Temuco, quite near to her stepson Bob who had managed the Mission farm at some time. Canon William Wilson was a widower when she married him and she had no children of her own. However, she had an enormous adopted family, was very good at giving hospitality, and would help anyone. Country people would often stay with her – especially the poorer ones. One person who lived in her house was José, who had a clubfoot and sometimes did a few odd jobs, and errands for her. Antonio Villarroel, the lay preacher who befriended us, was an agriculturist with the Chilean Ministry of Agriculture, also lived with her. Antonio travelled around a lot with his job so wasn't at home very often. Struggles used to teach English and had a class of nuns from the Catholic University meet in her house. At other times she would spend a few days in the country in her own wooden caravan. This was just like the old gypsy horse drawn caravans, with a rounded roof and made so that it could be moved if necessary. Whilst staying in the caravan she would spend her day helping the Indian women with their reading and writing.

Prison Visiting

Struggles also played the large harmonium used for the church services in Temuco. When she was in town I would normally walk to her house and then we would take the bus to visit the prison together. One day I knocked on the front door several times but she didn't seem to be at home. I wondered if perhaps she was ill so I walked round to the back garden calling her name. Eventually I

Struggles' house in Temuco

heard her voice and looking up, to my astonishment, saw she was standing up on the roof at the back part of the house. I was scared stiff and didn't want to distract her so I finally shouted 'Come down for goodness sake, you'll fall!'

But who will repair my roof?' she replied. 'I need a man and there's no one else here!' I walked away saying I refused to speak to her whilst she was up there – she was a very brave and caring old lady but she could be extremely stubborn! Struggles eventually lived to be over 100 although latterly she could not speak due to a stroke. She was very much loved by everyone!

As we visited the prison I could see everyone seemed to know her, calling her 'Granny Struggles'. The guards chatted with her like an old friend. They were not going to stop me entering when she explained I was a new boy and had no pass or anything. The outer wall was about 16 feet high and the prison occupied a whole block – most towns and cities are built on a block system in Chile. There were towers with guards on duty at each corner. It had been built for 350 prisoners, but there were over 700 men there! Once through the large gates and two inner barriers we walked down a long corridor. On the left we were shown into a patio, and the door shut behind us. At once we were surrounded by a group of youngsters mostly young teenagers. 'Granny Struggles' they all shouted in Spanish – they were so pleased to see her, and asked her what she had brought for them. This time I think she had some homemade jam, in small Nestlé's coffee tins, known as the "Purple Peril" by some people, because it always turned a mauve colour. In the winter she would bring the boys pairs of woollen gloves she had personally knitted.

Usually the routine was that Struggles would hand out old Christmas cards with choruses she had written on by hand. The boys would have a good sing and finally Struggles told them a Bible story interspersed with questions. She was a wonderful teacher, and the boys listened attentively. Weeks passed until one day she said to me, 'Now I am going away for a few weeks to stay with my step daughter in Concepcion, so I want you to continue visiting on your own. You'll be all right – the boys love you!' That was true, but whatever would I do after we had sung a few choruses? Once again I was scared stiff and began to pray desperately. On returning to the office I decided to talk to Sheila Baughan who was working as Mission Secretary. Sheila was good with children and suggested I borrow some old filmstrips with a small projector to take to the prison. So I translated the Bible stories into my simple Spanish, and got someone to check it for me.

I arrived with fear and trepidation at the prison the next week. Once with the boys I did everything as I felt Struggles would have done, and got through reasonably well. Lastly I got the projector set up and the boys all crowded round with expectation. But what I didn't anticipate was that the lads then started to read my Spanish notes, and could read them faster than I could! Just before I could get out, someone came up behind me and began going down my pockets. I was sweating profusely and was extremely pleased to leave and get back home again!

Walking home one week by the prison wall I could smell something burning. Looking round there was no one following me smoking! I was wearing a light coloured raincoat, having had my new overcoat stolen in the customs. Continuing to walk along I put my right hand into my pocket, but 'Ouch!' I pulled it out very quickly. One of the boys had dropped a lighted cigarette inside the pocket and it was burning through the lining!

There were 20 boys inside the prison, the eldest, who was 19 had killed his mother with a large stone. Most of them were in their early teens, but one day I found two little lads who were aged seven and eight years old. I discovered the police had picked them up for vagrancy having found them asleep in a lorry. The boys had also been selling chickens that didn't belong to them in the street market! One of them was called Sergio, and once I had his home address I set out to find his father's house. He lived on the outskirts of Temuco and the address was difficult to find. With my limited Spanish people didn't seem to understand me, but on the other hand people knew I was a stranger, were suspicious and must have wondered what I wanted! Eventually I opened a wooden gate off the street and found myself in a patio surrounded by single-storey timber buildings. There were a few muddy puddles where it had been raining, and a couple of free- range chickens scuttled out of my way. Over in the right hand corner I could see there was an open door. Stooping down and peering into the darkness, at first I could see nothing. Then calling out I discerned the faint outline of an old man lying in bed with a large number of old blankets and coats thrown over him. He was Sergio's father who had been ill for some time, whilst the little lad had been fending for himself, as there didn't seem to be a mother.

I also discovered that there was a grown up daughter working in Santiago who sent money home. Some time later a nicely dressed young lady came to our house, introduced herself as Sergio's sister and thanked me for my concern for her brother. She told me arrangements were being made to get Sergio and his friend out of prison and into a children's home. Fortunately this seemed to be the case as both boys soon left prison and I never saw them again after that.

The adult prisoners had quite a lot of freedom and would pass you walking in the corridors. I never felt afraid of any of them and one day I saw someone whom I thought I recognised. He was standing in a doorway so I went up to him and asked, 'Weren't you in one of the country churches I was taken to a couple of weeks ago?' I remembered clearly I had taken a photograph of him with his wife and small son. 'Weren't you one of those who were converted that day?' I continued. Adamantly he responded saying 'Oh I only stood up because I was asked if I believed in God!'

Another day inside the prison, on my way to see the boys, a man stopped me, 'Are you a Pastor?' he asked. I replied emphatically 'No, I am just a missionary!' 'Ah but it's the same,' he insisted! I tried to argue but my Spanish wasn't good enough. Anyway he was not to be put off, and went on to say that until recently the men in the prison had a regular weekly Bible study. Unfortunately for them the Pentecostal Pastor who normally led this had been promoted to Bishop and then moved to Santiago. 'So we have no one to lead our Bible study and we want to ask you to help us' he continued. 'But I can't speak Spanish' I protested! To which he quickly responded, 'How can you say that? You're a man of faith aren't you? Well then the Lord will help you!' He told me he would meet me the next week at the inner entrance, and they would pray for me in the meantime! However did I get into this situation, I thought, and then immediately began thinking how I might get out of it. Walking home along by the prison wall I began to pray frantically. Surely there were other missionaries more experienced than me who could do this? Over the next few days I asked around, but finally found it all seemed to depend on me.

Then I began to think that surely there were such things as Bible correspondence courses. Perhaps they could use one of those? In the end I turned to Sheila Baughan again and to my surprise she said there were some copies of a Bible correspondence course called 'Abundant Life' in the office cupboard. Apparently they were printed in Mexico and had been in the office a long time, 'So you might as well use them up', said Sheila. The first week, after being introduced by the leader, I then handed each man a sheet. I explained they were to fill in the answers and I would correct them next time. During the next week I continue to be very scared and prayed frantically, but still wasn't sure how this was all going to work out. The second week I found myself facing a large group of 40 earnest looking men all ready to go! I read out the first question and then pointing to the man at the front on my left asked him to read his answer. If the answer was right I would say "O.K."; if on the other hand it wasn't I would point to another to read his answer, until we got the correct one. In this way I wasn't saying much, and they seemed happy as they were getting their Bible study. However on the third week came the next shock! I discovered that normally they received 'laying on of hands' for the sick each week, and this had not been done for three weeks! It was announced therefore that they would now ask me to do this at the end of the meetings! I shook my head to say I couldn't do it, no one had shown me how to do it! Anyway I was a layman, and clergymen were the only people allowed to do that! I shrugged my shoulders

68

and just hoped their leaders would take the initiative the next week and do it themselves! Leaving the meeting that day, however, I couldn't forget the look of disappointment on their faces – I had another problem!

During the next few days I went out to Maquehue to see Pastor Herminio. With my limited Spanish I asked if he could accompany me to the prison next time for a bit of moral support. He was too busy, he explained, 'But you're O.K, why do you need me?' I explained it was really this problem of 'Laying on of hands'. Finally, he said with a grin, 'Right, I'll come with you next week to show you – but there's one condition - the following week you can do it on your own!' Herminio fulfilled his promise and so the work in the prison continued. Soon several men said they had received healing after the laying on of hands from week to week.

At other times I would be asked to visit the sick ones who were too ill to get out of bed. This meant going into the galleries where the cells consisted of small cubicles like concrete pigeonholes. The floor area of these measured about six feet long and four feet wide; they were eight feet high and built three storeys tiers, one on top of another, the only access being by climbing up a vertical metal ladder. Most of the prisoners had turned their beds round so that the end was suspended out over the walkway below, as this provided them with more room space.

Prison Life and Services

The men were allowed to work in seven workshops in the prison, depending on their trade. You could get an incredible number of things made in the prison, from saddles to sideboards, silver and copper trinkets and ashtrays, guitars and virtually anything. Several times I went with orders for dining-room chairs and churches would ask me to get them guitars made. On one occasion a missionary had a complaint so I asked him to come with me to the prison. The master guitar-maker was called to the barrier, and the person explained that the guitar kept going out of tune. 'Here let me try!' said the guitar-maker, and even without tuning it he began to play expertly with great speed. 'Well I can't see what's wrong with it' he said, and handed it back to the man's stunned embarrassment!

Brian Skinner had some excellent saddles made there for the farm. Usually the saddle maker would write out a list of the materials he needed and send me to buy them at a shop near the railway station. I learnt that Romanian-style saddles were considered best, followed by Chilean and then English ones.

During the Wednesday meetings I learnt so much from those Pentecostal Christians. The next thing they taught me was a different way to pray. Arriving at the door you were conscious of a hum of different voices. As the door opened all forty of them were on their knees praying out loud! This was not corporate prayer with everyone saying the same words – no, every man was saying his own prayer using his own words! As a member of the Church of England I found this really difficult to cope with – I just found it impossible to think or concentrate with such a hubbub going on. I decided the only thing to do was to apply the theory that if you can't beat 'em, join 'em! So getting down on that hard concrete floor, with the stony bits sticking in my knees, and the cold winter wind blowing through the glassless windows, I began praying my own prayer out loud! Why not - the Bible never said we shouldn't! Indeed it's quite possible that the early disciples did it this way at times, especially if you read some of the prayers in the book of The Acts of the Apostles!

The prisoners who led the service were very committed mature Christians. One man especially impressed me with his sincerity and like most of them he had a family. He had become a Christian since being in prison and was very concerned that all his family should come to know the Lord. He would sometimes hand me letters to post in which he urged them to repent and give their lives to Jesus. He knew he was going to be in jail for a long time, for I think he had killed somebody whilst under the influence of drink when doing a robbery. He was a gentle man with no hatred in him, but only a genuine repentance and love for the Lord. I found I had no fear of any of them, even though there were no guards present. There was another man who had been stealing his boss's cheques – but didn't seem to think that was particularly wrong. He would lead the service sometimes. This he did with great enthusiasm, and would frequently pause and shout out "Alleluia!" Often this didn't seem to have any relevance to what he was saying. 'Do you know why he does that?' one man said to me. 'He has an impediment in his speech, and sometimes can't get his words out, so when he can speak again the first word he always shouts is Alleluia!'

At one stage the men asked if I could help them lay a timber floor over the rough concrete in the room they used as a chapel. Generously my old Boys Brigade Company sent money to pay for this. The prisoners promised that if timber was delivered to the prison they would carry out the work, and they were as good as their word. Sadly, however, a few weeks later the governor confiscated the room and turned it into a tailoring workshop. I had a couple of meetings with him to try to work out a compromise, suggesting the room could still be used for prayer and services lunch time. His argument was, 'Well, you believe that God is everywhere - so why don't you meet in the patio?'

The Christian men in prison taught me so many new things. Later I was able to see that this had been very much part of my training for things to come. However, at that time in no way could I ever imagine what the Lord was preparing me for, but I will tell you about that later!

Spanish Steps with God's Spirit

Still struggling with my Spanish one day I talked again to my friend Pastor Herminio, as we travelled together cramped up in the back of the Land Rover. The vehicle was full of patients from the Maquehue hospital going for check-ups at the regional hospital in Temuco. At the time this was the only vehicle the Mission had, so the farm had to share it with the hospital, and it also had to be available for the Superintendent. There was the old farm lorry kept going by the loving care of David Merino, the Pastor's brother, but this was only used for short journeys and for carrying big or heavy loads. As we sat opposite each other in the Land Rover I felt I must take this chance to tell Herminio how frustrated I still was. I had been reading again the last chapter of Mark's Gospel so I said 'I see there that when Jesus sent out His disciples He promised they would speak in new tongues! Do you think that is a promise for me?' Herminio replied confidently saying, 'I'm sure it is; I have been praying for you that God would enable you to speak Spanish and I'll continue to do so'.

Later I began to have a few Spanish lessons with Marion Morrison. Reg Bartle, our Superintendent, had suggested that I prepare about three short talks and get Marion to check over my Spanish. I complied with this but really didn't feel very happy about it, because I couldn't imagine I would ever use them. Reg, however, encouraged me assuring me that once I had done this I could go out on Sundays in the Land Rover and visit some of the country churches just north of Temuco. David Merino was a licensed Reader, and the principal driver of the Land Rover. On Sundays David would leave Temuco with several people, dropping them off at various points to lead services in the country churches. I had never preached in my life, although of course I had given a few Bible class talks, but none of these had been in Spanish!

Eventually I was due to go out one Sunday morning, so read through my talk over and over again on Saturday night. By now it was 1.30 am and I was so tired and really fed up, having no enthusiasm for the task. Finally I decided I must go to bed. As I got to the foot of the stairs and put my hand on the handrail it seemed as if an inner voice was saying 'Go up and start studying Spanish.' Until then I had not had this sort of experience very often! So entering my little study room at the top of the stairs I looked round and there in the corner was my copy of 'Teach Yourself Spanish'. It was still lying on the floor, where I had thrown it six weeks before in utter desperation, still open with the pages face down, and the jacket uppermost all covered in dust. I picked it up, and after blowing off the dust, decided to write a list of six words. From then onwards I would carry a list of verbs or important nouns everywhere with me, out walking, on the bus or anywhere. Every week I would write out a new list, keep it in my top pocket and read it frequently. I have reflected several times as to what was happening at that time. I am sure this inner voice was the Holy Spirit motivating me to learn the language and fulfilling the promise Jesus had brought to my notice that His disciples would "speak in new tongues" (Mark 16). Since working in the prison I had also seen people healed when they had been prayed for, something quite new to me but the very things I had read about at the end of Matthew and Mark's Gospels!

On board the Reina del Mar I had watched the others in our group romp through their Spanish books, getting more and more chapters ahead of me. I found this so depressing, feeling I had no aptitude for languages, and only consoled myself knowing that they had all studied languages at school or university. I also tried to comfort myself thinking of all the time I had lost at school through illness, being in hospital and when our house was bombed. Finally I thought 'Anyway we never did any languages at my schools, so what hope is there that I will ever learn the language!' Yet now I could no longer use such excuses for it was undeniable that the Lord was performing miracles in my life, and I was seeing new things happen to me that had never occurred before.

Boys' Hostel

Still the Lord had not finished with me and was about to present yet another new and unexpected challenge to Ann and myself. The boarding part of the school in Chol Chol had to close as government grants were now five or six years in arrears. To help the pupils continue their schooling it was decided to provide hostels in Temuco for as many as possible. This meant that Ian Morrison, who had been Head of the school, and his wife Marion who had also been a teacher came into Temuco to run a boys' hostel. A hostel for girls was also installed at the Mission Centre at the side of Holy Trinity Church. Ann and I were to work with Ian and Marion in the boys' hostel. But first we had to find somewhere large enough for seventeen boys, two married couples, three children between us, the school cook, plus Ann expecting Stephen! Perhaps we had forgotten Jesus' words 'With God all things are possible'. For eventually a bungalow was found with a large garden, a small orchard and an out-building in the back garden. It was called the house on Holandesa Avenue and was owned by a Dutch gentleman and his wife who had imported and sold good quality dairy cattle from Europe. Later the couple had moved to Santiago where they were members of Saint Andrew's, the English- speaking Church.

The whole adventure ultimately panned out for our two families, although we had to work at it. Here I must add that Peter and later Stephen were to become bosom friends with Danny, David, and Nina, the Morrison children. We soon all got on like a big happy family and the students were very friendly with our children. At the beginning Ian decided to convert the upper floor of the timber barn in the garden into the boys' dormitory. The owner had originally used the building for cows whilst waiting to sell them. Ian was a great gardener and the soil was very fertile so we used to grow lots of our own vegetables. We also had about eighteen hens and a cockerel – plus a pig called Petunia who had the run of the back garden. The boys' parents would sometimes bring in farm produce and meat to pay for the board and lodging in kind. My job was to water the asparagus every day, and because the boys wouldn't eat it Marion used to send one of them down to the street market to sell it.

Everything was carried out on a very tight budget and we ate the same food as the boys. They, however, wouldn't eat salad, and refused liver as this was only considered fit for animals. Each morning two large baskets of newly baked rolls were delivered to the front porch before the boys' breakfast. As long as the bread was freshly baked that morning they would eat it. However, they never ate butter or margarine, so if the bread wasn't fresh they refused to eat it and would leave it on the table before rushing off to school. Country people didn't eat jam or marmalade, and tended not to eat puddings, so the daily menu was fairly frugal. The school system was such that the younger boys would go to school in the mornings and the older ones in the afternoons. Some of the older ones would go to evening classes and they came back between eleven and twelve o'clock at night. Most of these older ones had part-time jobs, usually doing domestic work in private houses during the daytime.

One day we woke up to find half the front garden submerged in about eighteen inches of dirty water and sewage. Too many people were using the system, and with all the extra water used for the boys washing, the septic tank was just not big enough. We got a man to dig a second pit alongside it but it was our job to get the garden cleaned up. So when the lads came back from daytime classes I told them they would have to help, or have no water and no toilet facilities, nor be able to get their clothes washed. They didn't like this and very begrudgingly moved the black sludge in wheelbarrows across the garden to the orchard. Although almost all came from farming families they didn't like getting their hands dirty insisting they were students! On another occasion one of the children had rammed a bread roll down the loo and I had to unblock it from the septic tank end, which was not really a plumbing problem!

A lovely lady from a Christian family who was a friend of the Morrison's used to help Marion with her children. Guillermina had a brother called Nelson who used to come in from the country to Temuco for evening classes. Our families were living in an interesting commune for in addition to the chickens and Petunia the pig roaming round the garden, we often had Nelson's horse tethered at the back of the house as well.

Let me include just one more rat story. Behind the kitchen there was a small upper storey and a lobby with wooden steps up to a small room over the garage. I used this small room as a study and had a wonderful view of the hills around Temuco. I was always interested to watch as they turned from green to a light brown colour during the hot summer months. The small lobby was really a larder where sacks of flour, beans and lentils were stored. It was also of course a place the rats loved to get into. María, formerly the school cook, was getting fed up with the regular incursions of rats into this area, and appealed to me to do something. Buying the largest trap I could find I placed it high up on a shelf. The next problem was that even though it caught the rats they just walked off with each trap with their legs caught in it. One of the boys suggested I tie a string to the trap so the rats couldn't run off with it, until that was the day when I heard Maria screaming at the top of her voice. Rushing through the kitchen, there I saw a very large rat with its nose caught in the trap swinging backwards and forwards like a pendulum. Suspended helplessly from the ceiling it was dripping a trail of blood right across the floor and into the open sacks of pulses. The rats always fascinated me with the way they could scamper vertically up the walls, and then run upside down across the ceiling of the garage where we kept the firewood. They just never fell off!

There was also a lovely little puppy Peter and Stephen were very fond of until one day when the boys were coming home at lunchtime two called me to say I should go outside as they thought the puppy was lying in the road. Sadly we discovered someone had left the front gate open and the poor little thing had been run over.

Family group – Temuco 1964

Whilst we were helping with the hostel Ann gave birth to Stephen in a clinic in Temuco. The boys, especially the younger ones, were thrilled when Ann brought the new baby home and they welcomed him with great curiosity. Our Silver Cross pram was very useful as this sort of thing was not available in Chile, so Stephen spent a lot of time enjoying the fresh air in it in the garden. 'Auntie Ann, Auntie Ann, the baby's crying' shouted Danny bursting into the house one morning. Going out to investigate I eventually found the pram out of sight around the side of the house. It was upside down with the wheels still spinning and no sign of Stephen. Slowly turning it up the right way I found him still strapped in and suspended by his harness hanging head down! He was fine, no harm had been done, and he soon stopped yelling. Danny was enthralled with the baby and loved taking Stephen out for 'walks' in the garden. Another day he came into the house holding Stephen by one arm and one leg saying 'Auntie Ann, the baby's crying!'

Seasonal Pitfalls

The Holandesa Bungalow was in a very sad state of repair. One big problem was that during the winter months, almost every time it rained all the all lights went out! This was because the rubber insulation around the electric wiring was perished and the leaks in the roof caused the lights to short circuit. The plumbing was pretty antiquated too – with most of the water pipes suspended on bits of wire under the house! Later we installed a wood burning sawdust stove in the lounge to make it warmer for the boys to do their homework.

A timber yard gave us free sawdust if we collected it and a canister of sawdust would burn for about forty minutes. The stove radiated a tremendous heat and glowed red hot with a bright cherry colour, except we found the big disadvantage was that the heat burnt the varnish off the furniture, causing it to come out in large blisters. Unfortunately the sawdust stove wasn't really a good idea!

In the winter in Temuco it often rains for weeks on end! The Mapuche Indians are generally quite short in stature, and I was captivated to see the men with their umbrellas and rubber galoshes hurrying along in the rain. Most of them would otherwise have to wear their 'mantas' (ponchos), which were hand woven from sheep's wool. The natural oil in the wool made them fairly waterproof but they could get very heavy when wet. At that time there was no alternative as there were no raincoats to be purchased in Chile. Often there would be large holes in the pavement and of course these filled with water. On one occasion we saw a small boy fall into a hole with water up to his armpits; fortunately he was all right and managed to scramble out again.

In the hot summer the earth road in front of the house produced clouds of swirling dust when motor vehicles drove past, and in the house we often had a coating of light brown dust over everything. One day our neighbour across the road, in his kindness, decided to pour old motor oil all over the road to keep the dust down. A little after this we began to discover black marks and oily footprints all over the carpets and polished wooden floors in the bungalow. This was so annoying with so many feet trudging in and out that we told everyone to use the back door.

Bernardo

Our extended family included Bernardo Avila, who was older than most of them and completely paralysed. Previously he had spent many months in hospital. Until he was eleven years old he had lived with his old widowed father. Each day he would be sent out early in the morning to look after the animals – but one day he did not come home! He had been struck down by a high fever and was lying on the ground unable to help himself; I think he was left in the open for at least two nights. Eventually two American missionary ladies visited his house and discovered that Bernardo had not been home for three days! They quickly went in their vehicle found him and took him to hospital. Very sadly the doctors said they could do nothing for him, and asked why they hadn't brought him earlier. Bernardo had suffered rheumatic fever and all his limbs had become set at the joints. His knees were fixed in a bent-up position and his arms bent across his chest. Later he stayed for many months in Maquehue hospital, and through the loving care of the nurses and the ward services held each day he came to know the Lord. He had a powerful voice and loved to sing hymns, and read his Bible avidly. During the time when the Bible Institute was held at the farmhouse he was invited to teach there. The Institute students would often take him to lead services and preach in the country churches.

When Bernardo came to live with us he had a single room under the boys' dormitory, on the ground floor of the barn at the back of the house. He always had a great fear that when there was an earthquake the boys would run out of the building and leave him on his own inside! He lived with us for over two years, and some of us would usually wheel him up to Church on Plaza Smidt for the services. My friend John Hollingsworth and friends at St John's Blackheath, together with members of my old Boys' Brigade Company, bought a proper wheelchair for him and had it sent out by ship. Prior to this Bernardo had to use a basic and very uncomfortable wooden cart – without any springs. Occasionally I was able to take him out in the country by Land Rover, where I led the service and he would preach.

Once Bernardo and I went to Nehuentue, a small fishing village on the coast. Here the children in the church listened spellbound as Bernardo was speaking, and after the service they all crowded round his wheelchair. The thing that most fascinated them was what was under the blanket that covered his twisted legs? As always Bernardo was delighted at their interest, and engaged them in animated conversation!

On one occasion I asked if a meeting could be arranged in the prison patio and I took Bernardo to preach. His strong speaking and singing voice was just what was needed and quite a big crowd of men gathered and listened attentively. When Bernardo had finished there was absolute silence, but then an angry voice from the back shouted 'How can you be so happy when you are completely crippled?' I waited to see how Bernardo would reply. 'All right, look at me and my twisted body' he said. 'But you see this is only a shell, and one day perhaps soon, I shall go to be with the Lord. Then I shall no longer need this body and will leave it behind – what about you?' Having got to know Bernardo whilst he lived with us, we asked him to be godfather to our son Stephen

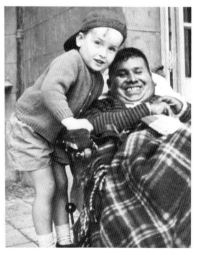

Stephen with his godfather Bernardo Avila

Later Ann and I were asked to run the girls' hostel and so we moved to the Mission Centre near Plaza Smidt, at the side of Trinity church.

Reg Bartle, our Superintendent, now felt it would be good if I was trained for Readership, and be licensed to lead services and preach. Following this I joined the training class with several Chileans including Bernardo and Panguilef Longcomil. Panguilef was a delightful and mature Christian schoolteacher who suffered many years with tuberculosis. He was son of a Mapuche Chief and later worked in the University com-piling a course in Mapudungu, which is the language of the Mapuche Indians. Later when we moved to Santiago he would often come on holiday with us. I was eventually licensed in the Temuco Church, kneeling

Zoila (15) in Temuco with Peter and Stephen. Outside the Girls Hostel

between Panguilef on one side and Bernardo in his wheel chair on the other. I remember this vividly because after the bishop had laid hands on me I was unable to stand up. I have to say this was nothing to do with the Holy Spirit; I just discovered I was standing on my scarf!

Too Trusting?

The Hospital in Maquehue had been damaged in an earthquake two years before we came to Chile. Once we had re-laid the drains it was decided to build two new wards adjacent to the old ones. I carefully drew up the plans with the advice of the nurses. We would build covered walkways joining the old building with the new, plus a larger kitchen. The new wards would have large windows for maximum sunlight and wide covered balconies outside for shade, and protection when it rained. Later the nurses asked me to make the windowpanes smaller as glass was expensive to replace, bearing in mind the frequent earth tremors. At this time, apart from the boys' hostel I would have to get out to the hospital twice a week to supervise the construction work. I tried cycling out once but I usually waited for a lift in the Land Rover. Amongst the carpenters was one called Raúl, who had been a student at the Alliance Bible Institute and was a committed Christian. He seemed to be a dependable person, so on his suggestion I appointed him as foreman. He was also able to explain my drawings and specifications to the workman, which was such a great relief whilst I battled with my Spanish. Raul also suggested that to save me having to pay out the men he could do that, to which I agreed.

The work seemed to be going reasonably well until one day one of the carpenters called at our house. He surprised me by handing me a brown paper parcel; this was a present he said because he was leaving and going to work in Santiago. I was extremely interested to know what was inside, and on unwrapping the parcel discovered a whole suckling pig. He was disappointed to be leaving saying that the wages weren't very good on the hospital contract and mentioned how much he was being paid. I was puzzled as the rates I had agreed with Raúl were much higher than that! Later I challenged Raúl and found he had been underpaying the men, because he had to pay himself more for his 'extra responsibilities!' What he was saying was that he was in fact supervising the workmen, and phoning me occasionally to ask for extra materials, etc. Yet he had never explained this to me. Later I discovered he had also cheated his church when treasurer. I lost quite a bit of money because of this episode, and was learning especially not to be so trusting in the future! Maud Bedwell was the Mission secretary and lived with us, so I discussed my problem with her. She was a wonderful missionary of the older school, had a very caring nature in every way, but was very correct and meticulous. She was responsible for the accounts, and in no way would she refund the money I had been cheated out of – that was my responsibility!

Another problem I had to contend with was the disappearance of building materials, especially timber and cement stolen during the night! Some of the nurses became rather agitated with me and insisted that I stay at the hospital overnight, but I felt what we needed was a night watchman. However, the new wards and other work on the hospital were eventually completed, to my great relief and general satisfaction!

Drunkenness

One of Chile's greatest problems was drunkenness and I still reflect on the effect this had on so many people's lives. On cattle market days in Temuco people would come into the town to sell animals. After selling an ox or a sheep the owner would find himself in possession of a large wad of notes. Then followed a great temptation for him to celebrate with his friends before returning home. On the earth road out of Temuco there were several small bars with a rail outside where customers could tether their horses, like those seen in cowboy films. It was not uncommon to see one of these small farmers lying in a nearby ditch, his head buried in his sombrero, sound asleep! Some of them would be left to sleep there until the morning. The saddest part was that these men would eventually arrive home not only in a pitiful state, but having had all their money stolen whilst they were inebriated! Miraculously the more fortunate ones would manage to keep in the saddle even though intoxicated. This was not due to any great feat of horsemanship, but rather to the ability of their faithful steeds steadying them, and keeping them in the saddle until they got home!

We were soon coming to the end of our tour and due to go home to England. We had done a great variety of things – but very little building work. I had designed a few churches as the Chilean government had promised to allocate a site for a church in every new housing estate. Later, however, a new government decided that these plots were available but would now have to be paid for; so the buildings never materialised! There was a possible site for a temporary wooden church in one area, but on visiting the site I found the ground was extremely wet and soggy. Local people had laid down a bed of wood shavings to soak up the water. The whole site was unstable and moved under us as we walked over it, and in my judgement was quite unsuitable.

Furnishing the Santiago Centre

I also spent several weeks in Santiago to help make furniture for the new Church Centre as the contractors were reaching completion. Arriving with a few hand tools I was taken down town to look at some pews in an old Presbyterian Church, which were quite ornate with curved ends. From a practical point of view, to make pews like that was just out of the question, because with no power tools I needed to make them as simple as possible! Despite this it was decided that the Presbyterian style was what was wanted! Even more frustrating we then had to wait for several weeks until a couple of lorry loads of 'Manio', an excellent hard durable Chilean pine arrived.

Lewis Jowett had done a great job really, because he had persuaded firms who used to buy their woodcutting machinery from his company to donate the timber. He was a Director of a company called Rhab Rochette. Lewis was a very good friend and a Reader at St Andrews the English church and had many useful business contacts. On arrival, to my astonishment all of the planks were much thicker than I had ordered, so I spent literally days and days planing them down by hand to the required thickness. Lewis also acquired us several carpenters' benches to work on. Unfortunately the benches turned out to very be badly burnt and were black and charred; they had been rescued from a fire in a furniture factory. However they were the only ones we had!

Talking about Lewis, I remember a discussion once arose about preaching in the small country churches in the south in the Temuco area. Lewis insisted that as we were Anglicans we ought to arrive at these churches wearing our cassocks (a long black buttoned up garment worn in church) and preferably our white surplices as well! After a pause someone asked him if he had ever tried riding a horse in a cassock? No more was said after that!

During this time in Santiago I became good friends with an Australian clergyman called Greg Blaxland, and we spent many long hours working together making the pews. As we stood waist deep in shavings in the evening, often the dulcet tones of Greg's wife Judy could be heard, calling over the upstairs balcony (a bit like Shakespeare's Juliet), 'Gregie, supper's ready!' After many weeks of hard work and much frustration a senior member of the congregation came to our aid by getting the pew ends cut on an electric band saw. In the refrigerator factory where he worked was a Pentecostal Christian friend who got permission to stay on and do this after work. In the end as it was still taking weeks to get the work done it was finally decided to ask the Methodist Industrial School to make most of the pews in their workshops. I was so exhausted and relieved at this decision, although I did manage to make an octagonal pulpit and a platform with Communion rail around. The first services were held in the Santiago Centre using the carpenters benches covered with coloured rugs, plus an assortment of dining room and kitchen chairs.

Joseph and His Dream
After staying many weeks in Santiago, Ann, Peter and I eventually returned to Temuco once again. Back in the south I was asked to go up to Chol Chol to estimate the cost of a new roof to the school. Sometimes staying there in the winter I would look out of the

bedroom window at the night sky. Of course being in the Southern Hemisphere I soon discovered that here was a whole lot of stars I had never seen before. Local people explained to me that most nights, looking up at the stars, you could quite easily see the "Three Marys" at the back of the school.

Working at the hospital constructing a new toilet I got the chance to work with José Cabezas. José (Joseph in English) was a church leader and a very kind and godly man. For many years he had worked as the hospital handyman and had a great deal of practical and local knowledge. He asked me to advise them regarding the water tower that served the local community but had been damaged during an earthquake. Most of the structure was quite sound but there were several bad cracks in the concrete tank at the top causing it to leak. Discussing this with José I said we could fill these with neat cement. "Do you know what they have sometimes repaired these cracks with?" he asked me. I had no idea and said so. 'Well horse dung!' he said, 'Because it contains very small particles of straw, so that when most of the dung is washed away the small particles of straw swell and fill the cracks!' This was obviously not what I would have recommended for a community's water supply, but it worked and that was the important thing!

José was a much respected church leader and was ordained a couple of years later. Every year the churches held a conference for leaders and about this time José had a dream. In his dream several church leaders met to plant some seed in a plot of ground they had bought. Those present with José were Herminio Meriňo, Ian Morrison and other known leaders. One of them tried to dig the ground with a spade, but the ground was just too hard so another tried a pickaxe, and someone else tried a long pointed metal bar! It was useless. Nothing would break up the ground. The leaders looked at each other not knowing what to do next. Then they saw a person approaching them in the distance. He asked them what they were doing and they explained they were trying to plant seed. 'You must wait for the rains of the Lord' he said, and then turned and disappeared again! José had this dream twice, and told it to Herminio at the conference. 'The Lord is speaking to the Church and you must tell the conference!' Herminio said. 'But they won't take any notice' José said. Nevertheless, Herminio insisted and José asked permission to tell the church leaders about the dream.

Some ten years later, whilst I was visiting in the south, José invited me to preach at the evening service in Chol Chol. Knowing I was coming, the headmistress of the school Señorita Nimia Rivas, asked me to tea before the service, and José called round afterwards to accompany me to Church. Sadly, I discovered that, although she used to play the harmonium, she had stopped going to church because she felt José lacked the education to be Pastor of the church! Arriving at church I was asked to sit at the front with my back to the congregation, until I eventually moved into the pulpit. I felt a great sense of God's presence as José's two sons led the singing playing their guitars. Then mounting the pulpit steps I turned to face the congregation and looked down the Church. I was absolutely amazed to see the whole place was packed to capacity! Of course some were pupils from the school, but on previous occasions the church had nearly always been two thirds empty! I began by thanking them for inviting me, but then said I was overwhelmed and asked them what had been happening in Chol Chol; and why were there so many people in church? The answer was, of course, that the 'rains of the Lord' had come and the Lord had poured out His Holy Spirit on the church, and José was beginning to see the fulfilment of his dream!

I have since come to understand, mainly from South American church leaders, that the coming of the Holy Spirit to churches has much to do with the quality of their leaders. Where they have spent much time in prayer and regular fasting the Lord has shown them what He expects of them! Sometimes they have had to wait for several years, and one of the verses quoted to me has been 'Call unto me and I will answer you, and tell you great and wonderful things you do not know.' (Jeremiah chapter 33, verse 3). This of course reflects in a negative way on so many church leaders and other Christians (especially in England) who are too busy to seek the Lord in this way!

Invitation to Return

As our first tour was coming to an end, I was gradually beginning to express myself in Spanish and get the gist of what people were saying. Yet I couldn't really see what there was for me to do in Chile! I had obeyed God's call and assumed I should return to my old job with the Greater London Council. I was quite surprised at this point when Rev Reg Bartle, our Superintendent, said to me that the Society would like me to return after a period of leave and visiting churches in England! Reg added that he felt I had become an all-rounder and would be personally disappointed if I didn't come back. Some of the American missionaries like Bill Strong, Head of the Centros Biblicos Mission, who had taken a personal interest in us as a family also said they hoped we would come back.

Here I need to express my very sincere thanks to Reg Bartle as he was so patient with me, helping me to cope with my feelings of frustration and disillusionment. He himself had a very difficult task as team leader, juggling so many different responsibilities. He had suddenly found himself thrust into the job of superintendent when Tony Barratt was sent to Paraguay. In my opinion all the stress took its toll on Reg's health over the years. One great problem was transport. At this stage there were two hospitals, one in Chol Chol and one in Maquehue, in addition to the farm, plus many remote country churches with only one vehicle. The farm did have a lorry, but it was on its last knockings and was only kept on the road because of the patient maintenance work of David Merino. Our new Superintendent Reg Bartle should have had first call on the Land Rover, but he could only use it about once a week and sometimes not even that!

In England Canon Harry Sutton was keen for me to attend a theological college and become a clergyman before returning to Chile. However I had never been keen on the idea of ordination and remember having conversations with Bishop Bill Flagg and Derek Hawksbee. Both had been students at All Nations College so I decided I would apply there and hope to study biblical and mission subjects.

Chapter 6
FIRST LEAVE IN ENGLAND

Once back in England things moved quickly and I went for an interview with David Morris, the Principal of All Nations College. On arrival at St Margaret's station I was not sure where the College was so telephoned for directions. 'Just hang on and we will pick you up by minibus,' Mrs Ann Davis told me. When I found the distance was only a mile and a half I declined her kind offer and said I would walk, wondering what sort of missionaries the College produced who needed to be taken everywhere by car!

David Morris was extremely helpful. He had been a missionary in the Sudan and had previously served as an army major training men for the African Rifles. This was quite controversial in those days as many thought the Africans were not intelligent enough to be soldiers in the British Army, which of course he proved to be absolutely untrue! David had been just the man for that task, and now as teacher and former missionary he was excellent as Principal of All Nations College. I still have a great admiration for him and will always be grateful for the advice he gave me. At the first interview the Principal surprised me by asking what I wanted to study. I assumed he would tell me and said so! 'Ah well, as you've been a missionary for four years I'm sure you have some idea of what sort of subjects would make you a better one!' he responded. So I decided to go for the first part of the Bible Diploma, plus mission subjects. He then told me Christ Church, Ware, had said they would provide us with a flat, so I went to meet the Rev John Bournon, the Vicar.

John was very helpful and showed me an upstairs flat that the church had recently refurbished, which was located at the top of the School Keeper's house. The flat was quite small with the bath in the kitchen, two bedrooms, a sitting room and a toilet installed in a large cupboard. The church had invested all the money from their missionary fund to provide this flat, and fixed the rent to tally with our SAMS weekly rent allowance which I think was £5 a week. Christ Church also provided all the furniture. People didn't have central heating in those days so we bought a large 'Valor' paraffin stove, to stand on the landing and heat all the flat. Of course, we could move it around if we needed to. One dark evening Ann and I arrived back home after shopping in London to buy new clothes and sleeping bags for Peter and Stephen. Someone had parked a car on the road outside the house, but we didn't give it a second thought. Mr Ager, who lived with his family on the ground and first floor, and was caretaker at the church school, then handed me some car keys saying 'These were left by a friendly clergyman!' The car was a very large 6- cylinder 1940's-style Rover.

It was a very dark winter's evening and getting into the driver's seat I tried hard to find where to put the ignition key. Suddenly the shadow of a large policeman fell across the windscreen. He informed us he had come to remove the car as the people next door had reported it had been dumped outside their house! He was extremely polite and asked me if the car belonged to me. I then related the very unlikely story that we were just home from South America and a friend had said he would lend me a car, and had obviously left it without stopping to show me how to drive it! The policeman then became very practical and said 'Oh I used to have one of these!' and began trying everything to see if he could to get the car started. In the end he came to the conclusion that the battery was flat. So together we pushed the car across the road to park it at the side of the church. There unfortunately, it had to stay for several weeks as we were strapped for cash and I just had no money to buy a new battery – all very embarrassing!

After some time an ultimatum was issued by the churchwardens that if I did not get the car moved they would! With trepidation one Sunday morning I watched through the curtains of our upstairs window for the car to be pushed away by the wardens and choir. Then, to my amazement and great relief, it didn't happen, because the Lord had all things under His control. Wonderfully, the next day I received a cheque for a few pounds in the post! On Monday evening I quickly went to buy a new battery and walked up New Street to collect it in an old pushchair. I had waited until after dark as I was too sensitive to ask anyone to collect the battery by car. Returning with the battery in the pushchair, I was coming round the corner when suddenly I saw a couple from church approaching. I was so embarrassed that I quickly slipped back around the corner, and hid in someone's front garden behind some bushes, waiting until they had passed! Reflecting on the new battery I must thank the Lord for He has always without fail provided for us in so many ways and on so many occasions!

All Nations College

Canon Harry Sutton had said that the Society had agreed to give me a year's leave to study, and would pay our rent and normal living allowance, but I would have to pay my own college fees. At that stage I had no idea how the college fees would be paid. Remarkably, though, during our four years in Chile we had actually saved sufficient money to pay my first term's fees. Over that period we had bought no clothes and had lived on a fairly frugal diet. One evening we had been invited out to supper at the house of some friends when I was called to the phone. It was David Abel, Captain of my old Boys' Brigade Company in Blackheath, saying the boys would like to pay for a term's college fees! I was embarrassed, and at first refused their kind offer, but Dave insisted saying I was their 'Missionary' and as an old boy they had already been supporting us, and would be very disappointed if they couldn't help! It made me feel so humble to think that these boys wanted to pay my fees, and so I finally accepted gratefully. I have to say that I really don't remember how the last term's fees were paid, but we were learning to trust the Lord who has never let us down!

Life at All Nations and living in Ware was very happy. Peter attended the Christ Church of England School, and had a wonderful and very caring teacher who was a member of Christ Church. I also made some good friends at college who were going to the Sudan, Nepal, South Africa and two pilots going with Missionary Aviation Fellowship to Chad. At this stage All Nations was still an all-male college although the wives did have the opportunity to go to certain lectures and Ann managed to attend those.

Because of my building knowledge I was sometimes asked to help with maintenance jobs. I was informed one day that one of the estate cottages, occupied by a student family, had a chimney that did not function properly. Every time they lit a fire smoke would billow down into the house. I explained that a cowl was needed (not spelt cow) and I offered to fix it. Because of my sense of humour I think some people possibly thought I was kidding. So the rumour was put round that I was intending to get a cow on the roof! However, once in place the cowl certainly cured the smoke problem!

Another afternoon I was detailed to fix some metal posts in the kitchen garden. Tom Paget supervised the maintenance programme at the college and told me to use a bag of cement and some ballast I would find in the potting shed. A student called Paul, a pilot and prospective candidate with the Mission Aviation Fellowship, was told to work with me. It was winter, extremely cold and heavy frost had made the ground as hard as iron. Paul suggested that perhaps it would save time if I dug the holes and he mixed up the concrete. Being so cold we were going to be glad to get the job finished. Task completed, we washed and went off to get our tea. During the meal Tom came into the refectory - he was a bit flushed and obviously angry. Then in a rather agitated voice he gave out a notice about basic building classes! This didn't register with me and I carried on eating. What I did not know was that unbeknown to me Paul had gone into the potting shed and used a whole bag of Tom's expensive compost instead of cement to make the concrete! Tom was absolutely beside himself and turned on me saying 'Call yourself a builder – pah - tomorrow you can both go back and dig the posts out and start all over again!' Despite this incident Tom and his wife Marion have remained very good friends ever since, and we have stayed with them in their cottage several times!

During our year at Ware Ann's dad used to come over to see us from St Albans and we would go over to visit him in 'Freda'. The boys wanted to call the old Rover by that name as, although I had suggested Fred, they insisted that all cars were female! Two important conversations ensued with Ann's dad whilst living in Ware. He was thinking of getting married again as he had been on his own since Ann's mother had sadly died of cancer when Ann was only nineteen. The other conversation was concerning our return to Chile. Dad challenged me 'Why on earth return to Chile, you've given up a good job and a pension?' You've got two children now, so you must think about your family!' I got on very well with Ann's dad, but it seems he had never got over the disgrace of having a son-in-law who was a missionary! Ann would still not be persuaded either and remained steadfast, which must have been a great disappointment to him. During this time we had a great holiday with my parents in Dymchurch.

To Chile Again

Soon it was time for us to return to Chile. My mum and dad came to stay while Ann worked for a few weeks in a bank at Hoddesdon to get some extra money, and I used to pick her up after morning lectures. Each morning she would leave home before the postman came.   One

*Dymchurch 1966. Ann, Granddad, Aunt Helen, Aunt Edie, Grandma,
Stephen and Peter*

morning a letter had arrived from our new Superintendent, the Rev
Douglas Milmine. Our orders were not to return to Temuco but to
come up to Santiago, the capital. As it happened, Ann had experienced
an extremely frustrating lunch hour that day trying to buy curtain
material for all the windows in the Temuco Centre. There must have
been at least twenty windows, and there just wasn't that amount of
material in the shops! Ann got into the car and began to talk to me
about her fruitless and frustrated saga. Until, that was, I handed her the
letter from Doug Milmine! I remained silent to let her read it! Ann
usually takes most things in her stride, so after a few minutes she
reflected and said, "Ah, now I can see why the Lord stopped me from
getting all those yards and yards of curtain material!"

The return journey was to be by ship from Tilbury to Lisbon and then
on to Buenos Aires. We arrived at Montevideo in a very thick fog
and could not dock as it was impossible to see. All day long a loud
gong was sounded from the back of our ship, which I believe was the
Arlanza, to prevent other shipping from colliding with us. Eventually
we disembarked in Buenos Aires, but not before realising I might
possibly have a problem with the customs. The day before I was
called to the Purser's office to sign a customs declaration form.
Surprisingly I was informed that amongst my baggage in the hold was

a crate containing Land Rover spares. The Society had not advised me of this and the crate had travelled the whole journey in my name without my knowledge. As I was going through the customs shed the officials became very agitated, accusing me of importing car spares, which was apparently illegal! I tried to explain that the spares were for the hospital Land Rover in Southern Chile. 'Anyway, the spares are in transit and we have no intention of unpacking them in Argentina,' I said in desperation. Finally after 'In Transit' had been painted on the packing cases they were locked up in an enclosed store until we could get them loaded on the Trans Andino train going to Chile a few days later.

Our train journey took about forty-eight hours travelling across the Argentine Pampa, with me sleeping on the floor because for some reason they had only booked us two beds. During the whole journey sand was seeping through our sleeping compartment doors and windows, covering everything with grit and dust until we arrived at the Chilean border. Before boarding the train for San Felipe we had to pass through customs. They were so insistent that we could not bring any kind of fruit into Chile with us. Actually we had about six oranges for the boys to eat on the journey. Of course they didn't want them, so I sat down and consumed all the oranges myself in the customs! Eventually after a long slow horseshoe-shaped route though the mountains the train arrived at Mapocho station in Santiago.

The Land Rover spares arrived safely and a few days later were on their way by lorry to Temuco. In the customs hall sorting through our boxes some days later I discovered a number of our tea chests had been broken into. In fact one containing a new sewing machine had a hole the size of a football driven right through it from one side to the other. Unluckily for them the hole wasn't big enough to get the sewing machine out. Unluckily for us, there were quite a number of new dresses missing from our luggage that were being sent out for some of the single ladies. I quickly wrote home to make an insurance claim. To my great horror and consternation I then discovered that the friend who had kindly promised to insure our luggage had not done so! When I enquired why, he came out with the astonishing excuse that he thought the premium was too expensive! We tried to compensate the ladies for the loss of their new dresses, as they were obviously very disappointed; however I suspect they were incredulous about the reason.

Chapter 7
SANTIAGO AND THE ANGLICAN CENTRE

The Anglican Centre in Santiago was an impressive nineteenth century mansion built by a man called Letelier. He was a Civil Engineer and a member of parliament and had built it as a family home. It was three storeys high with over 50 rooms and had a beautiful maple parquet floor in the hall, which was used as the church's worship area. Most of the rooms overlooked the two streets below, either Cienfuegos or Erasmus Escala, as the building was situated on the corner of both streets.

The Anglican Centre in Santiago

Nearly all the windows consisted of glazed French doors opening onto small balconies, each enclosed with an ornamental wrought iron balustrade with figures of dragons. On one occasion, when Stephen was really fed up during the church service, an older member called Francisco Antiqueo gave him his keys to play with. After everyone had gone home Francisco came to our flat upstairs to pick up his keys. We couldn't find them anywhere, so the poor man had to go home without them. About six weeks later we found the keys

93

dangling from the balcony railings on the first floor, suspended over the street below!

Downstairs there were also some fascinating plaster figures of climbing monkeys on the walls. Across the hall was an impressive mahogany staircase leading to the upper rooms around the balcony overlooking the church below. Also on the ground floor was the Mission office, one used by the Superintendent and sometimes occupied by Bishop Howell's secretary. At the back of the worship area was a coloured stain glass window overlooking the patio. Other ground floor-rooms included the church parlour, several rooms used for English classes, a flat where we lived during our first year and storage rooms along the back corridor. Ann and June Harrison ran these English classes, which were quite successful with business people and others. On the first floor were three flats, some guest rooms and there were extra rooms up on the second floor. These rooms on the top floor were often used by schoolteachers who came to Santiago to study at the Summer School under the Ministry of Education.

Ann's English Class, Santiago

Our main assignment in Santiago was to run the Centre together. Ann cooking for the many visitors, changing beds and washing bed linen, and both of us responsible for hospitality generally. My other job was to be pastoral assistant, which meant visiting members of the widely dispersed congregation, and being responsible for the maintenance of the building.

During the evening service on our first Sunday I was asked to come forward to say a few words. As I looked around I immediately became aware of several missionaries who were accustomed to preaching and leading services. Amongst others in the congregation were English speaking visitors from South Africa, Germany and America. Some of these were professional people, while others were doing research, but all tended to be people who preferred to come to services in Spanish.

Standing at the front there I felt rather overwhelmed by this august assembly, so I decided to keep my opening words very brief. In my best Spanish I tried to say something like 'I have come to work in this vast city feeling I am not a very gifted person but I am prepared to do whatever God wants me to!' Apparently my words gained full marks for humility, however Bishop Ken Howell came up to me. He thanked me for my words and then went on to say 'You are of course completely wrong about not being a gifted person, and shows you don't know your Bible!' I was a bit stunned yet strangely I didn't feel put down. Ken had rightly reminded me that Jesus taught His disciples that He expected them to use their gifts in the parable of the talents (Matthew chapter 25). He then continued 'every Christian has at least one God given talent. St Paul also teaches about the gifts the Holy Spirit gives to Christians to enable them to serve God.' I need to say here that this was nothing to do with the Charismatic movement of which I knew very little, having left England in 1962. Yes, I already knew the Holy Spirit was at work in me in a new way, motivating me to learn Spanish and enabling me to do things that I had never done before. I was being alerted to the fact that the Lord had more challenges ahead for me. Perhaps Ken knew more than I did. Anyway very soon I was about to go into another steep learning curve in my Christian life.

On arrival, in addition to the many visitors, there were the Gibbs and Ortiz families living in the Centre. There were also at least two single missionary ladies.

People in the congregation included missionary families or visitors. Of the Chileans members about 50% were Mapuche Indians who had migrated from the south to work or study in Santiago. Pastoral visiting was enormously time-consuming as it meant taking two or three buses across the city (with a population of two and a half million people) just to see one person or family. I had been licensed as Reader in Temuco but I was only to lead services and preach occasionally. Little did I know, however, that all that was to change very soon!

An All Purpose Building and its Problems

Because of my building experience there was the responsibility for the maintenance of the Centre. There were five bathrooms, five kitchens, plus extra toilets, and the five large gas water heaters that were always going wrong. One heater in the Gibbs' flat kept going out so Doug Milmine decided that the pilot light could be improved by ramming a large nail into the thin copper tube to increase the flow of gas! This certainly improved the gas flow, until unexpectedly there was a loud explosion and part of the artefact was propelled across the kitchen and embedded in the wall! Rene Gibbs, who was in the kitchen at the time, was at first very pale and quite speechless. However, regaining her voice Rene appealed to me to never let that happen again, and to always get a gas fitter in the future!

So it was that we came to discover Señor Moya. He lived just down the road, and soon became a frequent visitor to the Centre, prepared to tackle most jobs. Anything from rescuing two baby rabbits lodged in a rain water pipe from our upstairs patio, to putting on his wet suit to tackle a major blockage in our drains. The drains were constructed when the house was first built and ran under the basement, making them almost impossible to get at. For several days the basement was waist deep in sewage and smelly water! On inspection Mr Moya reported that it was extremely serious as the salt-glazed pipes were disintegrating and were blocking the connection to the main sewer in the road. Good old Mr Moya was prepared to do his best to remedy the problem. Anthony Smyth, who was living with his family in the Centre, said he was prepared to help as well. Mr Moya donning his wetsuit immersed himself in the murky water. It was going to be a long job and without a pump. So we formed a chain with Mr Moya passing us the buckets of foul liquid, which we poured into the gutter in the street opposite our kitchen window. At five o'clock we were feeling quite relieved at a job well done. As I was washing I was suddenly alarmed to find the police at the front door asking who was living in the building. 'Do you realise you are breaking the law by pouring this raw sewage into the street?' they exclaimed. They then gave me an ultimatum saying we had half-an-hour to hose down the gutters with disinfectant and clean it up.

There were, of course, a number of other problems with such a large old building that had never been properly maintained for years. In the roof space was a large storage tank providing us with water. Often the water in the street was cut off at the main or the water pressure was very low. Therefore, with our own large storage tank we always had water in the building. Unfortunately the galvanised pipe that supplied the tank came through the church and passed up the side of the main staircase. Normally this made no difference even when the pump came into operation, although it always made a very loud vibrating noise. That, of course, didn't matter too much when there were no services in church.

One Sunday evening Bishop Ken Howell was due to preach during the evening service. Somehow the pump seemed to be in a bad mood that evening and have a grudge against the poor gentleman. Suddenly, just before the sermon as Ken moved into the pulpit, the pump kicked in with the most horrendous noise, similar to a team of pneumatic drills. Now it became absolutely impossible to hear or think as the pump did its worst. Bishop Howell, who was a quiet unexcitable man, just stood there waiting patiently for the pump to stop. The minutes passed and the pump still refused to stop, almost as if it were conducting its own alternative service! Finally the episcopal gentleman bellowed in a loud whisper in English, 'John for goodness sake turn that confounded thing off!' I was very much averse to doing this because normally the pump had a mind of its own and would often not start again afterwards. So against my better judgement I complied with the orders of my superior and moved quickly to turn it off. Dare I add that of course the 'confounded thing' wouldn't start the following morning!

Obviously this large old multi-purpose building had its disadvantages, but as we lived upstairs there were a few benefits. During the service on another Sunday Omar Ortiz was celebrating Communion and passed me the chalice. As I took a sip of wine I realised at once the liquid had turned rancid! I wanted to vomit as it reached the back of my throat, but waving my hand to him I took the chalice. Then running quickly upstairs to our kitchen I spat the liquid down the sink. Next, opening the fridge I then discovered that we had no wine! An English merchant sailor had consumed the last drop when given private Communion during the week. Frantically I began rummaging through Ann's cupboards until at last I found some red jelly crystals. Quickly dissolving them with a little warm water I filled the chalice with cold water from the tap. With all possible speed I then ran downstairs and handed the new wine back to Omar! Everyone was still reverently kneeling in prayer with eyes closed, and so to my knowledge no one ever found out!

The New Lay Pastor

We had arrived in October when there were three clergy on the Centre staff – but by February they had all gone! Omar Ortiz was transferred to a new church in a housing estate at Renca. Eddie and Rene Gibbs's son Stephen suffered badly from asthma and doctors advised them to live nearer the coast where the air would be better, so they moved to Quilpue. Doug and Ros Milmine returned to England and later Doug was appointed bishop of Paraguay! The pastoral crisis in the congregation did not really concern me as I presumed the powers-that-be would appoint a new pastor. Then out of the blue I had a phone call from Bishop Kenneth Howell – 'John, the Church Council have approached me to ask if I would appoint you as Lay Pastor of the congregation, and I'm happy to do that!' I couldn't believe it – I wasn't ordained and was only a Reader – and anyhow, how could I do the work of three clergymen, in addition to all the visiting I had been doing?

As I seriously considered the Bishop's words I thought why not ask one of the other people who were members of the Santiago Centre congregation, several of whom were at that moment involved in theological teaching and student work. If these wouldn't take on the job, with all their degrees in New Testament Greek etc, they were still going to continue to be members of the congregation! So as I thought about being the pastor of the church it became an increasingly daunting prospect and gave me a great sense of inferiority! I was absolutely astounded that Bishop Howell had even considered asking me! However, after my appointment some of the missionaries did continue to help with the preaching and others with the all-age Sunday school.

Later I continued to reflect on the variety of reasons why no one else was available to be pastor. It was certainly true that there were fewer clergy! As quickly as I could, after making my decision, I called a special meeting of the Church Council to discuss matters. Since receiving Bishop Howell's phone call I had thought and prayed about this situation and my mind focused on two young men in the congregation. Both had leadership roles in the church; Florentino led the Youth Fellowship, and José was Superintendent of the Sunday school. I explained to the Church Council that in no way could I possibly do the work of three clergy and a Reader; if they wanted me to be pastor I needed their co-operation and full support. So I asked if these two young men could help me in leading services and preaching occasionally. They agreed and Florentino was prepared to preach once a month, although José was reluctant to do so as frequently! Bishop Howell would allow me to baptise people, most of whom were adults who were always baptised in the river. Available clergy would celebrate Communion once a month, especially Tom Curtis and Omar Ortiz.

New School

Before Doug Milmine and his wife Ros left they were extremely kind to us as a family. They suggested we get Peter into the English-speaking school, which their boys had attended, and kindly gave us some shares in the school. Craig House School was some way from the Centre and meant we had to travel by two buses to get there. Stephen was really too young for school but was so keen to go. One morning, because he often refused to eat his porridge, I promised that when he did eat his porridge he could go to School! I have to confess that I have never seen anyone become so suddenly converted to eating porridge, and from that time onwards he was a reformed character. So we then enrolled Stephen in the Nursery Class and I used to take both of them to school on the bus each morning.

The boys made some good friends at their new school and were invited to several birthday parties! At that time Dinky toys or matchbox cars were unobtainable in Chile, so the boys were very popular with their school friends as they usually gave them these as very rare and expensive presents. Their friends were really fascinated when they came to our enormous house – all fifty rooms with its own tower! Soon they put it around the school that 'The Jacklins lived in a castle!'

Callers at the Door and those Looking for Work

Many of the church members were extremely poor, having come up from the south and only able to get domestic jobs or work in bakeries on shift work. Those who lived near the Centre would sometimes ask me to help them move house. Because many only lived in one room this would involve loading up their few bits and pieces into the Mission Volkswagen and taking them to their new abode. Knowing I was the main driver on one occasion an older member asked me to take his aged father back home to Temuco after he had come up to Santiago for medical tests. Whilst in the capital they had discovered he had cancer, but because of his age felt it was best if he returned home without treatment. He was a gracious old gentleman, and the son offered to pay for the petrol if I would drive him back to Temuco, some 350 miles south. Although I had to drive back the following day, I felt it tremendously worthwhile. The old gentleman was so grateful and I was surprised and delighted to discover later that he actually lived for several years after that and was so pleased to be back home once again.

Many people would travel up from the south by train to the Central Station in search of work. On arrival some of the men would wait around at the entrance where employers looking for unskilled labour would take them on. Others would go to stay with relatives, but still others would come to the Anglican Centre. Our system was to provide bed and breakfast on the understanding that they went out looking for work during the day. I would send them out early to buy a morning paper, and when they came back I would go through the adverts with them. We also had lots of callers each day asking for money or food. Ann would always prepare more food than we needed so that it could be heated up for them, or we would provide sandwiches, bread, cups of coffee or tea, or second-hand clothes. Unfortunately not all of our visitors were genuine.

One day a man asked for a pair of trousers and a jacket, saying he needed them to start a job. Looking down at his trousers I asked what was wrong with the ones he had on. He showed me that the seam had come undone. When I suggested it only needed stitching he became very aggressive and said, 'And how do I get that done then?' When I turned back my lapel and held out a threaded needle he was even more incensed! Looking at my jacket he said 'why can't you give me the one you have on?' I knew he would never believe me if I explained that I only had one other which was my best one. In the end I opened my jacket and showed him that the lining was all hanging in tatters and that the coat was virtually worn out!

Then there was the incredible story of the Canadian concert pianist. One afternoon the English Chaplain Rev Graham Jack phoned to warn us about this man. Within the hour a large man with a black beard, and smart dark suit arrived at the Centre. He explained he needed a large sum of money to fly down to Punta Arenas where he would board a Chilean Naval vessel. The ship would then sail to a point within Antarctic waters owned by Chile, and there on board he would proceed to play his piano where no other concert pianist had ever played before! 'What's wrong with sailing from Valparaiso?' I asked him, as this was the main naval port and only 70 miles away. He explained that this would mean waiting several weeks for a ship and that he was running out of time! He insisted that he was completely genuine and produced a glossy programme of concerts where he had played all over Canada! Yet I knew according to my information he wasn't all that he appeared to be and we were being ripped off every day! I had no way of getting the money he wanted, and I have no idea whether he got to Punta Arenas or not, and that was the last we saw of him.

At this time Sheila Baughan, now working as the Bishop's Secretary in Santiago, said she was concerned that increasing numbers of people were asking for money at the front door of the Centre. This was strange and she wondered if it had something to do with me. I didn't argue but became determined not to give money to anyone. I decided that I would try to visit more of the families of those who came asking for help. I found that a number of callers were of course quite genuine. Such as the man who needed food for his family, and whose wife was ill and was nursing a new baby and living in a small shack. Arriving at their home I found the wife was seriously ill with tuberculosis, so I not only gave them food but also money for medicines. It was usually extremely difficult and very time-consuming to sort out the genuine ones. Money given at the door could most probably be spent on cheap wine. Consequently when callers asked for money for their train fare to Temuco I suggested they jump in the mission vehicle and I would take them and buy a ticket at the station. I felt quite pleased with myself at this and thought I was winning. That was until I found out that the shrewd ones would wait until I had left the station and then sell the ticket to someone else!

One day Ann attended to an old gentleman who came to the door looking wet, bedraggled and very distressed. He said he had been sent down to us by someone he'd met in the street who'd asked him why was he crying. He apologised profusely and said he didn't want any money or food – just a length of cloth to wrap the body of his young granddaughter in before it was released from hospital.

One of the regular clients at the Centre we called Fatso - an enormous man weighing some eighteen stone. He was one of a group of seven men who slept each night on the marble landing at the top of the entrance steps to the Centre. I would sometimes come home after dark having been out visiting church members. On arrival I would have to step between the figures sleeping on pieces of cardboard and covering themselves with old coats or newspapers to keep warm. Getting home late one night I found all the lights had been turned off so I couldn't see to get my key in the lock of the outside door. After successfully opening the outer door I still had to unlock the heavy inner door. Struggling to open this I turned to see Fatso grinning with an uplifted bottle balanced to bash me on the head! I shall never know whether he was joking or not but I certainly didn't wait to ask him!

A few days later it was my turn for little revenge. Raúl a pastor's son, and a student who helped as assistant janitor, came in to say he was unable to clean the front steps. Fatso was refusing to get up and just lay in the porch grinning. I have the feeling that Fatso was possibly mentally ill in some way, and he was certainly very unpredictable. Appealing to him I explained we now needed to clean the steps down after they had all finished their breakfast! The office would soon be open for the day's business and visitors would be arriving. The big man just grinned and said something like, 'Well I'm not moving – you make me!' Then the Lord gave me an idea. I asked Raúl to bring out the hose we used to water the flowers and turn the water on. Turning my back on Fatso I then began washing down, moving my broom closer and closer to him. After a few minutes I looked round at Fatso's patch and to my delight I found he had already gone - beetling off with his cardboard boxes and bundle of newspapers to store them safely in the manhole ready for the next night's bed and breakfast!

Cheap wine was the cause of so much distress at this time and many of the poorer people would drink too much. I once asked one of the men who slept in the porch why he drank so much? He replied 'if you had just enough money to buy a meal, or a litre of cheap wine, which would you choose?' I said 'A meal of course!' He then said 'Well I prefer the wine because sleeping rough in the winter is so cold and I just can't get to sleep. A litre of cheap wine inside you warms you up, and you can get at least three or four hours sleep!' Sadly he told me each day early in the morning he went up to the freight yard at the railway station in hopes of getting a casual day's work, but was nearly always unsuccessful.

One day we had a caller named "Valdivia" he explained this wasn't his proper name but a nick name people had given him as he came from the southern city called by that name. He had come to Santiago some years before, had worked very hard and had a job as an official in a large trade union. He was very well paid but with the pressure of work he began to drink. In the end because of the drink he lost his job, and couldn't get another one. Being desperate he decided to seek out his brother whom he knew was headmaster of a school in Santiago. Valdivia found his brother who gave him some money to help him out. After some time he went back again, but this time his brother said he was a great embarrassment to him and never wanted to see him again! Our caretaker and I listened to his story and agreed that if he would stay off the bottle we would give him free board and lodging and he could work in the church as assistant to Don Andres. Valdivia agreed so we brought him in, made him strip off his smelly shirt and clothes, and between us gave him a good scrub in a nice hot bath. Afterwards we gave him a complete set of clean clothes and put him to work. Things went well for three or four days until coming back one afternoon Don Andres told me Valdivia had gone missing and he had no idea where he was! Later in the afternoon I found him sitting on the kerb with two old drinking friends opposite an off-licence half a block away! That was the last time I saw him.

Sometimes if a person genuinely wanted to kick their drink problem I would contact Alex Hughes at the Salvation Army. They had a centre for alcoholics where these men earned their keep by working in the laundry. Unfortunately there were only about twenty places in the centre and they were almost always over-subscribed.

Chapter 8
LIFE IN THE CITY

Alcoholism and Crime

During the course of hospital visiting I was asked to visit the husband of a very faithful Church member called Nolfa. They had only been married about eight weeks when he was rushed into hospital with cirrhosis of the liver. He had a drink problem and sadly he died within two weeks. Visiting the psychiatric hospital I saw some very heart-wrenching sights. At times patients were so ill with advanced cirrhosis of the liver that they were unable to eat. Often there would be a number of plates of food left over from the day before still on the lockers at the side of their bed. One good thing President Allende did was to address the problem of alcoholism by prohibiting the production of cheap wine. The better quality wine was less damaging to the liver and being more expensive the poorer people couldn't afford to buy so much.

I did hear one great success story about a man with a drink problem. It was getting near to his birthday and his wife and family were becoming more and more worried that on the big day the man would drink himself senseless. Being committed Christians they turned to their local Pentecostal Church for support. By the time the birthday arrived the man had got quite a large number of bottles of liquid refreshment in ready to celebrate. Somewhere around 7.00 am on his birthday, whilst the family were still in bed, the first callers from church came to congratulate him. They brought a number of small presents and goodies, but of course no wine. Having seen his guests out he began to think about opening a few bottles. But after he shut the door, suddenly another group of Christians turned up to wish him a happy birthday with a few presents and of course no wine. To the man's great consternation the constant stream of Christian visitors continued all day, so much so that by the end of the day he had not been able to consume a drop! I can't tell you whether got over his drink problem or if he became a Christian, but his wife and family just praised the Lord for answering their prayers.

I have been greatly influenced by the lives of Chilean Pentecostal Christians who would generally never drink alcohol and I have felt personally that if I did I would be letting them down and be a bad example. Drunkenness so frequently ended in fights and caused an enormous amount of suffering for wives and children. I therefore have to confess, and make no apology, that my experience in Chile has only led me to remain a teetotaller. Where a man has given up the bottle, not only has his life been completely changed, his children have been better clothed and fed, and family life has been completely transformed! Referring to Jesus' miracle of changing water into wine someone once said 'In some cases Jesus has even turned beer into furniture!'

Unfortunately Chile also had a reputation for pickpockets. During our first year we had to travel from Temuco up to the capital and at one stop decided to get out of the coach to have a cup of coffee. We never gave a thought to security and quite happily left our outer coats on the seat of the coach assuming they would be safe. Not until we arrived at Santiago did we discover that our passports were missing and realised they must have been stolen whilst we were off the coach. Consequently we then had to wait for more than eighteen months before the British Consul would issue new ones!

Later on we saw several people get money stolen on buses. Some friends were getting off the bus during a holiday at the coast. The wife stepped off first and then the husband leaned forward to hand the baby to her, unfortunately as he did so a wad of notes was whipped from his top pocket.

Santiago from the Japanese water garden on San Cristobal Hill.

One afternoon in Santiago I was waiting for the traffic lights to change. Suddenly a man squeezed in between my vehicle and the car in front and sped off down the street with someone's wallet. As he weaved in and out of the traffic he left a whole trail of small coins jumping and bouncing behind him, just like some runner in a paper chase.

Sitting sleepily on the bus in the Alameda on another very hot summer's afternoon, and waiting for it to move off, suddenly I was awakened as to my amazement a hand slipped through the open window and snatched a gentleman's spectacles off!

The Mercurio (the national daily that is nearest to the *Times*) ran an article one morning with full size photographs with the caption 'School for pickpockets'! It showed pictures of pick pockets on work practice taken by a secret camera from inside a shop window in the city centre of Santiago. A brilliant shot showed a small boy quietly sneaking up behind a smartly dressed businessman briskly walking to work. Moving with great speed and lightness of touch he lifted up the back of the man's coat. Still holding the coat with one hand he then removed the wallet from the man's back pocket with the other. The operation was quite painless for the man never felt a thing! Other photos showed a group of boys meeting together on a derelict site in the city centre sharing out the morning's takings! Santiago had a reputation for excellence in training some of the best pickpockets in South America.

One night during our first year in the Santiago Centre, whilst living in the ground floor flat, we had intruders during the night. Coming into the kitchen in the morning at breakfast time we found the window to the patio facing the street hanging wide open. The evening before Ann had decided to make jam and now there were plums all over the floor, mixed with the contents of two broken bags of sugar. Worse still we then discovered that all sixty of our long-play records were missing, plus the record player. Ann's purse and house keys, with some small change had also gone, although we later found these on the floor behind the cooker. It would seem that the felons had been interrupted because the kitchen wall clock had stopped at 3.00 am. They had fled leaving the clock behind on the worktop in their hurry to get away. On reflection we realised that Stephen had woken up coughing at about that time, so he must have scared them off!

Our neighbours reckoned that if we were to find our precious records they could probably be found on sale in the Persian Market near the Mapocho railway station. Ann was determined to do all she could to get them back as they were records we had had since before we were married. The Persian Market was an interesting place selling all sorts of stuff from car spares to saucepans, including tools and electrical goods. Ann made several fruitless journeys there, but we never saw our records again; they must have been snapped up quickly if they had been there at all!

Fall of Man

On a lighter note I remember the occasion when it was decided to have a party for some new expatriates coming to work in Santiago. Ann had spent many hours preparing food, such as jellies, trifles, cakes, sandwiches etc. Just before the guests were due to arrive Ann noticed a bulb in the chandelier had burnt out. 'It's so dark in here; put a new bulb in that for me, please', she asked. Now the ground floor ceilings in the centre were thirteen feet high and I had no idea where I could find a pair of steps tall enough to reach the chandelier. The enormous dining table had two centre leaves and could seat a large number of people. Because time was short, using my initiative I decided to place a dining-room chair on top of the table. Carefully placing the chair legs between the eatables I was soon up on top of the table and mounted the chair. All was going well until I felt the chair moving. Unbeknown to me, one of the centre leaves in the table was loose and was slightly tilting to one side. So with my weight the leaf slowly began sliding to the floor leaving a large sagging gap in the centre with no support for the tablecloth. Next the plates began slithering gently down from both ends of the table into a large deepening abyss! Soon plunging plates and eatables were cast into a giant crater, totally mixed up, with a good scattering of sandwiches strewn over the shiny polished floor. Hearing the noise Ann emerged from the kitchen to see me sitting on the floor amidst all the debris and destruction! The final blow came literally when the leaf toppled over and banged me on the head. Ann was at first speechless and was soon at the point of tears, until one of the American visitors retorted 'Ah gee let's just eat it off the floor!' Ever since that experience the phrase 'throw a party' has tended to stir up certain emotional and painful memories within me!

Into the Estates and the Shanties

On Sunday mornings during our first year in Santiago a group of Church members would meet in the morning at the Centre. After praying we then set off to lead a number of small Sunday schools in housing estates and shantytowns south of the city. At the end of the morning's activities we all returned to the Centre and Ann would feed us. There could be as many as twenty-two people sitting down to Sunday lunch! Sheila Baughan, who had worked with Francisco Antiqueo at some of these Sunday Schools, had asked if I could help. Christmas morning was something the children always looked forward to and they would greet us with great enthusiasm. After singing some Christmas carols together we then gave each child a small present and a packet of sweets.

Nuevo Centenario was one of these shantytowns located directly behind a big textile factory called the Yarur Works. The settlement was just a narrow strip of land with a railway line on one side and a dirty canal on the other. It was a terrible place where sixty families lived with quite a number of children. Most of the shacks were made of wood but some were only of cardboard and nearly all had tarred corrugated cardboard roofs. The thing that amazed me was the way the children were always so smartly turned out for school. Each wearing their own beige overall, the girls with a ribbon in their hair, and all with clean shiny shoes! At Nuevo Centenario two or three people were killed on the railway line as there was no fence to prevent people wandering across it. Loos consisted of makeshift privies precariously cantilevered over the canal, where the sewage went, as did all sorts of other rubbish. I arrived one day to see a pig swilling around in the filthy water. On another day I saw a small child miraculously saved as she was snatched out of the stinking water.

Toilets – Nueva Centenario

Yet it was here that Don Julio was the first to give his life to Christ and where several Church families lived. I will certainly mention more about Julio later because he was such an interesting character whom we came to love during our time in the Centre!

After we came to Santiago Reg and Thelma Bartle and family came up from Temuco to live in the Centre. Within what seemed a short space of time Reg had taken over from Doug Milmine who went to be bishop of Paraguay. Talking earlier with Reg we found that our mothers knew each other, and had only lived a stone's throw away from each off Charlton Road, Blackheath! During our first years in Temuco Reg had trained me to lead services and preach and prepared me to be a licensed as a Reader. Reg was excellent at preaching and teaching but I feel with all the extra responsibility of administration thrust upon him this took a toll on him. So roughly four years after arriving in Santiago the Bartles sadly had to return to England due to Reg's poor health.

Everyone in Chile has to be married in the Registry Office as Chilean law doesn't recognise the legality of Church weddings! Indeed our own our wedding certificate had to be translated into Spanish and stamped, signed and legalised by the British Consulate. Before this was done we were not considered to being legally married under Chilean Law. Consequently when Stephen acquired his first identity card, before he was three, it said that he was 'illiterate, unemployed and illegitimate'.

Visitors Galore

During our time in the Centre Ann was expecting Deborah. Life was extremely demanding for Ann as in addition to looking after our young family she had all the extra cooking, washing and hospitality involved in running the Centre. The week before Deborah was born we had a General Synod and a South African Youth for Christ team stay for ten days!

Thea Coates and June Harrison were very good 'adopted aunties' taking the boys to the cinema or to the swings or for walks in the park. Our friend Zoila Pranao also helped Ann as she lived with us whilst doing her nursing training. Zoila had always had a soft spot for the boys since she had lived with us whilst she was at secondary school in Temuco.

110

Amongst the visitors we had a rather bossy lady journalist. She had come out to do a report for an English Christian periodical, had experienced a stressful journey, and was a bit overwrought. She came during one of those times when lots of visitors were coming and going. Obviously the dear lady was longing to get to bed so we quickly arranged a room to let her get some rest. A few minutes after she closed her door there was suddenly a splintering of timber and a mighty crash. We were afraid to knock on her door knowing she was so tired and a bit tetchy. Unexpectedly next came a series of loud sobs and she was crying inconsolably. I realised that the dear lady's bed had collapsed and I have to confess I found myself quietly laughing with tears running down my face. I hasten to add that she was in no way harmed and we were much relieved to see her unscathed at breakfast the next morning.

One rather demanding English visitor came from Oxfam. He had been an officer in the armed forces and was used to having a batman. After breakfast he asked me if there was a shop where he could get a suit cleaned. I just didn't know if there was such a place in those days as that was something I had never contemplated. 'What's wrong with the suit? I asked. He replied 'Well it really only needs pressing.' So I took the suit and pressed it for him. The next day he asked if I could get some shoes cleaned for him. I just took them away and brought them back all bright and shiny. A couple of days later he asked me 'where did you get the suit pressed and the shoes cleaned?' 'Oh I actually did them myself' I replied, which I think slightly embarrassed him. He returned to Santiago three years later and we found this time he actually stayed in a posh hotel in town. The service in the Centre was obviously not up to his standard.

Ann's job not only meant preparing all the extra meals and changing the beds, but washing all the bed linen as well after visitors. When I was out she also had the added burden of frequently attending to the continual crowd of callers at the Centre front door. This meant Ann had to trail down two flights of stairs, and trudge right through the church to open it. Foolishly I had not noticed all the pressure this was putting upon her - until one evening, being several months pregnant with Deborah, she suddenly showed up in our bathroom with her suitcase packed. I had the boys in the bath with my back to her, but turning around I was startled to see her standing in the doorway. Ann had decided that she was so fed up that she was going back to

England! I could see she was in a very determined mood with her suitcase ready, so I knew there was no point in trying to persuade her otherwise. Fortunately the situation was saved as Ann didn't drive and she needed to ask me to drive her to the airport. By the time we had discussed things a little I was relieved to see she had changed her mind!

Ann was booked in to the Presbyterian Clinic to have Deborah as we were not covered by the Chilean National Health Service. In those days the husband wasn't allowed to be present at the birth, so I went to the hospital as soon as they would let me in! Arriving at around 7.00 am I was so pleased to see Ann, but found the delivery had not gone well. Soon, within a few minutes she became very distressed and blurted out that they wouldn't let her see the baby! Ann was convinced that something was wrong with the baby, so I quickly spoke to a nurse and said 'Could I see my baby daughter please?' Within a few minutes the lady appeared with Deborah in her arms, and to our great relief we could gaze on our beautiful bouncing baby! I must, of course, add that there was nothing wrong with her whatsoever!

The Linconĭrs

I often went out to the shantytowns on the rickety old buses accompanied by Enrique Linconĭr. Between us we were involved in Sunday schools and small Bible study groups in various places. Enrique was a competent self-employed electrician, yet often he could be out of work for weeks. As the eldest of several children he would send money down south to his widowed mother to help support his younger brothers and sisters still at school. By his example Enrique emphasised again to me the biblical principle of 'tithing,' that is, giving ten percent of your income to the Lord. When he had been paid for completing a contract he would come up to me in the vestry on Sunday evening. Calling me quietly aside he would thrust into my hand an envelope bulging with bank notes and say "Pastor this is the Lord's, I got paid yesterday but want to hand this tenth over immediately so that Catalina and I will not be tempted to spend it!" He would then add that his wife, who was also a very committed Christian, needed to do some food shopping as I suspect they had very little left in the larder.

The Linconĭrs had no children but were extremely generous, always ready to help others, and frequently gave hospitality to people who travelled up from the South. On one occasion a young man came up from the south to enlist for his compulsory military service. The day came when the lad finally left to report to the barracks. After he had left the house Enrique went into the bedroom only to discover that the trousers to his best suit were missing. Enrique realised his guest must have taken them with him.

Some of our contemporaries felt Enrique was not very gifted because he tended to talk so much. Yet the children really loved him and rushed to greet him when he arrived at the shantytowns. Enrique demonstrated over and over again such a great gift for generosity and love for people.

Enrique outside Nuevo Centenario

Graciela and Goliath.

Because some of our congregation lived in the Nuevo Centenario shantytown, Enrique and I began to visit them. Crowds of children always came out to greet us and flocked all around us when we

arrived. They loved to talk to us and ask us questions so we decided to start a Sunday school there.

Children living in Nuevo Centenario

Graciela, a lovely Christian lady living in the shantytown, soon offered to help us with the children's classes. Her husband was a bus driver and they had eight or nine children, all of whom were incredibly clean and smartly turned out for school each day. After a short while, in addition to the Sunday school, a group of parents used to meet with me in a large hut used for community meetings. All of this went well until, inadvertently, we upset the community leader who afterwards kept the meeting room locked up! The problem really started when Canon Harry Sutton came to Chile and I took him round the shantytown. The community leader was keen for Harry to take photos of himself, not just of the children! He was really conceited and was hoping this could give him a bit of publicity and show what a good community leader he was! Harry didn't respond to the man's request so he became very annoyed and punished us by locking up the meeting place.

One day Graciela told me this true story of how the Lord had miraculously answered prayer. It was late at night and the whole family was in bed together with her eight children, and her husband Goliath. At some time during the early hours of the morning she was woken up by a strong wind. With each new gust the cardboard roofing was being lifted up and then dropped down again. Graciela was convinced that any minute the roof would be snatched off and go sailing through the air. Even worse within minutes it was soon raining as well. Graciela told me that somehow this experience reminded her of the storm on the Lake of Galilee in Jesus' day. Now as the strong wind was lashing and lifting the roofing sheets, the rain was falling like stair rods. The children still remained asleep in their beds but Graciela was terrified. So slipping out of bed she quietly knelt by her bedside on the earth floor. 'Oh dear Lord', she pleaded 'all my children are sleeping and will soon be soaked to the skin in their beds. Please still this storm as you did that day on the lake. I know you can do it because you did it before.' Graciela continued on her knees for several minutes. Then after just a short pause, amazingly and miraculously the wind died away and the rain gradually stopped. Still on her knees Graciela could only thank the Lord and then slip silently back into bed!

Graciela was a very caring mother. Unhappily Goliath, her husband, had a drink problem and would frequently turn up drunk for work. He was a bus driver so sadly he eventually got the sack because his boss said a drunk driver was just too much of a risk to the passengers! Graciela was the first person in the shantytown I prepared for Confirmation. The problem was each time the Bishop came to the Centre to conduct a confirmation she never turned up. Eventually Jean Llewelyn went down to see what was wrong and to collect

Graciela. We then discovered that Goliath got drunk on purpose on these occasions so that his wife couldn't leave him on his own. Graciela was such a dedicated wife and told me that Goliath had previously fallen on the fire when drunk, so she would never leave him on his own in that state. Regretfully, in the end Graciela never was confirmed.

One Church member who lived in Nuevo Centenario was Francisco who had taught himself to read by reading his Bible whilst in the Army. One afternoon Goliath decided that he would like a Bible so as Francisco was reading his Bible he asked him to get him one. Francisco explained that this would cost him so much at the bookshop. At this Goliath became very abusive and tried to grab Francisco's Bible! A fight ensued, as Goliath was probably drunk anyway, and his glasses were smashed in the process! By coincidence I came on the scene as Francisco was on his way to the police station to make a statement, and he asked me to accompany him. I don't think the police did anything, but the incident was a very sad one as Goliath was very short sighted and couldn't see without his thick pebble glasses. After he lost his job, many friends who were taxi drivers had paid him to repair their taxis. I really found his drink problem all so depressing. The sad thing was that Goliath was a good and intelligent man when sober, but when drunk and now without his glasses he couldn't do anything!

Don Julio

It was in this shantytown we met the old gentleman we called Don Julio – we gave him the title "Don" as this is an expression of respect in Spanish. He was like a bag of bones, very pale, and had previously been ill with tuberculosis. Graciela in her kindness used to give him a cooked meal once day and he in exchange kept her supplied with firewood. Don Julio would be a tramp in English terms, but he was a loveable character and later became a very faithful member of the Centre Church. I discovered that he had been brought up in a Catholic orphanage and had no family. I found it quite moving when he sometimes spoke to me about 'the lady who could have been my mother' who used to visit him as a child. When he grew up he worked and lived on a farm where they provided him with food and accommodation.

Julio was always bringing me small presents and insisted on calling me 'Patron'. I was embarrassed and a bit irritated by this so I eventually told him I didn't want to be his 'Patrón' (Boss in English), or anyone else's for that matter. If he really wanted to call me anything, then please call me Pastor.

After Deborah was born Julio brought me an old mug, saying 'here is a present for the baby!' Another day I was in the process of laying a concrete driveway in the patio, so the mission vehicle could be parked off the road at night. When Julio found out what I was doing he became quite animated and said, 'Oh, I can get you several bags of cement for free!' Later that evening he took me across the main road and down a dark side street to where in a corner were stacked several bags of cement. On examination I could see that the bags were obviously left there for the workmen to repair the pavement the following day. 'To take them would be stealing from the local council,' I said, but Julio really didn't see it like that! 'But, Pastor', he insisted, 'the bags have been left over; look, you can see the work is all finished now!' I still wasn't convinced and had to tell him so!

On another occasion Julio arrived with a cardboard box full of small records, each one completely new and in its own dust cover. 'Could you help me to sell these please?' he asked me. The problem, he explained, was that if he tried to sell them people would think he had stolen them! Actually he had found them thrown out amongst the rubbish from some offices in the centre of town! Early next morning we went to the basement studio of a local radio station. The man we spoke to was quite polite but explained that the records were all marked 'Samples not for sale', so he couldn't possibly buy them. However as a goodwill gesture he finally gave Julio a small amount of money. As we walked home afterwards Julio kept on at me that I should have insisted the man give us more money and felt he'd been done! He took a long time to forget this incident, but finally forgave me!

Sadly one day Julio turned up in a sorry state; he had been beaten up and had bruises on several parts of his body and face. He had been involved in an incident in the shantytown. The dispute had arisen because Julio, now a Christian, had denounced two men for living together with the same woman. Unfortunately they were big beefy men and he was short and all skin and bone, and they had really beaten him up! What's more, they put enormous slabs of concrete on the roof of his little shack, so that he was afraid it would collapse, and they threatened to kill him if he came back! On the day Julio's case came up I called at the courthouse and handed in a letter I'd written verifying that Julio's testimony was true. I wasn't allowed in and the judge decided to postpone proceedings and call for a medical examination. Many weeks passed before this was possible, by which time, of course, all the bruising had disappeared!

Julio was absolutely terrified of the men who had beaten him up and really needed somewhere to stay for his own safety. We thought the easiest thing was to give him a room on the third floor of the Centre for the time being. He stayed for at least ten months and each time I

Peter and Stephen building Don Julio's new house

suggested he return to the shantytown he said he was too scared. Finally, I got some timber and corrugated iron sheets and with Peter and Stephen we made him a little prefabricated hut. It was illegal to build on the shantytown site so I engaged a man with a horse and cart to transport it there and I followed afterwards with my tools. It seemed sensible to erect the hut near to Graciela's house so that she and her family, with other Church members, could look out for him. Julio was delighted with his new little shack and as far as I am aware has continued to live there happily ever after!

Osorno Volcano and Petrohué River

Chapter 9
HOLIDAYS AND NEW CHALLENGES

During the long summer holiday we sometimes went to the seaside in the Viña del Mar area as this was only about 60 miles away, not far from the principle port of Valparaiso. Viña has beautiful sandy beaches, always kept very clean and is just right for children. Although the water is extremely cold, due to the Humboldt Current off the Pacific coast, swimming is not for the faint-hearted. We never had much money in those days. So for our first holiday since moving to Santiago we camped in a couple of classrooms in St Paul's School as the children were on summer holiday. Another year David and Mary Pytches kindly invited us to look after their house whilst they were away. Ann and I actually slept in the bed and even in the same sheets the Archbishop of Canterbury had just slept in! David and Mary had a small swimming pool in the garden, which David had dug himself. Of course, the swimming pool water was much warmer than the sea so the children really appreciated it.

Unbelievable Weather

One year we thought we really ought to go camping and explore the lakes in Southern Chile. Getting permission to use the Mission vehicle we headed down to the area of Lake Llanquehue some 600 miles south of Santiago. Reaching Temuco was about the halfway mark, then after several more hours we passed near to volcano Osorno. We didn't see much of her as she was covered with heavy mist up to her middle, like some giant duvet. Nearing the end of our journey we passed through the town of Frutillar on the edge of the lake. Travelling south around the circumference of the lake we at last camped at Puerto Varas. The lake is enormous covering over 540 square kilometres and is the third largest natural lake in South America. This large expanse of water is very impressive and looks just like the sea.

Arriving late in the afternoon we stopped to stand on the promenade just watching the wind whipping up the waves. Unfortunately, however, within the hour it clouded over and began to rain, something that never happens in the summer in Chile! The boys only had summer clothes on so very soon their shoes and shorts were absolutely soaked through. As fast as we could we got our tent up and then passed a very wet and windy night on the edge of the lake. We were really glad when it was time to get up but so depressed when we saw it was still raining. With the weather being so cold and miserable we soon packed up our tent and decided to move on. Later looking around the town we saw a house with a bed and breakfast sign next to the German Lutheran Church. The landlady was very kind, allowing us to hang up our wet clothes in her warm kitchen and spread out our soggy tent in her garage.

Large communities of German people live in this Southern part of Chile. Around 1850 the Chilean government invited them to settle there, encouraging them to farm the soil and engage in forestry. It's interesting to hear German being spoken in the streets and shops and see the German influence in the houses. The Lutheran Churches in this part still conduct their services in German. It also fascinated me to see the men ploughing the fields with horses. In most parts of Chile the small farmers, including the Mapuche Indians, plough with bullocks if they can't afford tractors.

We only stayed one night in the bed and breakfast in Puerto Varas. The next day the sky was still very overcast with more heavy rain showers in prospect. We were absolutely fed up, and had had enough. So we decided to make for home where we could at least get some warm dry clothes.

As we travelled north the weather continued to be very depressing, until, nearing Santiago to our amazement the sky cleared, the rain subsided and the sun came out. This cheered us up so much that arriving back home we quickly dumped all our rain-soaked stuff and speedily picked up dry things. Within an hour we had set off towards the coast near Valparaiso. Unbelievably we then had a very good week with lots of sunshine! We camped in a very dry leafy area under some large eucalyptus trees. The site was quite near to where we had attended church family camps on previous occasions. As soon as we got our tent up we began to sort out our stuff and discovered we had lost our toothbrushes. So for the next few days we didn't clean our teeth. Later back home looking at our holiday snaps we saw one showing Deborah deliberately 'posting' our toothbrushes in one of the water carriers!

Deborah posting the tooth brushes.

Other Vacations and Excursions

Another very memorable holiday was spent camping at the invitation of Bill and Agnes Maxwell. We travelled altogether in their Land Rover to an area somewhere north of Concepción. Shortage of space during the journey meant I was crammed in the back with all the boys and the baggage. Near the end of our journey, just after crossing a wooden bridge, we were surprised to see a wheel go bounding and bouncing past us. It bumped along at speed, veered to one side off the road and eventually ended up in the ditch! We had no idea this was one of our wheels as the vehicle was still travelling along at speed. Then all at once our vehicle lurched to the left and those of us in the back were all thrown in a heap on top of each other! One of our back wheels had come off and we had still been whizzing along on three wheels! No one was hurt, and this turned out to be one of the best holidays we'd ever had. It happened that a local farmer had seen us go past and knew we couldn't get very far on three wheels. He came out of his gate and very kindly invited us to camp on his land near the river. Our boys really enjoyed fishing and playing with a small rowing boat with the Maxwell children there, and the second week we moved on to another site by the sea.

Here we camped just a few yards up from the water's edge and were able to watch the fishermen returning home with their catch early each morning. The men went out in the evening just before dark and stayed the night on a sandbank. During the night the tide changed and numbers of large flat fish would be left stranded on the sandbank. Surprisingly, without any nets or equipment, the men were able to catch the fish with their bare hands! Being so near to the sea we were in just the right place to buy fish from the men before they took their catch to sell in the village. Also, living a few yards away was a kind lady who supplied us with fresh warm bread which she baked every morning.

The second time my parents came out to Chile we drove to the coast one day and called at a shop near the port of San Antonio to buy some 'empanadas.' These are like Cornish pasties and contain meat, eggs, vegetables, olives, and usually hot Chili peppers (called Ají in Spanish). Because granddad had to be careful what he ate we asked the lady if they were very hot. "Oh no I make them myself!" she replied in perfect English! Her name was Mrs MacDonald and was from a well-known English family in Santiago. She turned out to be a very kind lady and actually offered to let us stay in her log cabin in the woods at any time.

Later we took her up on this offer and stayed in the cabin for a few days. It was very rustic and miles from anywhere but great fun for the children. Round the back was a veranda overlooking a beautiful wooded valley. We had asked permission to use the Mission Volkswagen and parked it in the woods. An arrangement was made so that we could use the vehicle if we paid so much a mile towards the maintenance and of course paid for our own petrol. One afternoon I was startled to see the vehicle slithering down a slope through the trees with no one in the driving seat! To my relief the heavy undergrowth slowed it down and it finally it seemed to stop in a thicket between two pine trees! Running down I saw the children had been playing inside and one of the younger ones had released the hand brake. Actually Peter had had the practical presence of mind to pull it up! I shudder to think what might have happened otherwise.

Bumps and Punches

Santiago, being the capital is always extremely busy with traffic and the buses used to be very full. Occasionally I was asked to ferry people across town, and one day the Rev Omar Ortiz, who had been at a meeting in the Centre, asked me to drive him out to his church in Renca. As we approached the bridge over the Mapocho River, towards Recoleta, there was a long tailback of vehicles bumper to bumper. It was impossible to travel very fast so I was in no hurry to keep close to the vehicle in front. Suddenly, however, without warning a vehicle came speeding across the main road from my right, and tried to squeeze between our car and the vehicle in front! Scraping past at speed it ended up in the front of the Volkswagen, scratching the side of the other vehicle and ripping off its cover strip.

Immediately the two men in the cab leapt out accusing me of causing an accident! I wasn't going to get involved until they began demanding money to pay for the damage to their vehicle. Pointing to our vehicle I said 'And who's going to pay for the devastation you've caused to our vehicle?' For in fact we had sustained far more damage than they had. They continued to shout and swear and become very aggressive, at which point Omar stepped in front of me to protect me. Suddenly a punch swung through the air, striking Omar under the eye! He was knocked to the ground and I fell over his legs. Then like a flash the two men leapt back into their vehicle and sped off. Fights of this sort were very common in Chile. Generally drivers had no car insurance, because as it was not compulsory by law most of them didn't trouble. Wisely, however, all the mission vehicles were insured!

Omar's face was soon becoming very swollen and one eye was almost completely closed up! He really began to look a sorry sight and I felt I wanted to help in any way I could. "I don't know what Sonia is going to say!" he said. "Could you please explain to her how I got my face so badly bruised? And please could you possibly preach next Sunday because I can't stand up at the front of Church with a face like this?"

We realised afterwards the reason why the men were so angry was that their van was an Electricity Board vehicle they had borrowed during the lunch hour! I often reflect on this incident as Omar really took what was coming to me. It reminds me so much of how Jesus paid the price and took the punishment which we all deserved!

On our corner of Cienfuegos there were frequent collisions. On one of these occasions a small van crammed full with boxes of eggs was hit and slewed round by another vehicle. The van driver had great difficulty getting out because the door on his side was jammed. Eventually when he did manage to force it open he came out covered in broken eggs, some sticking on top of his head and lots more stuck on his shoulders and back. Fortunately he was only shaken and not badly hurt, but there soon followed a fierce shouting match!

One busy Christmas Eve a lady accompanied by her husband was crossing the road from the open market with two large bags of shopping. Suddenly I saw a bus accelerate and shoot forward sending her flying in the road. Her husband being absolutely beside himself wrenched open the driver's door and pulling him out by the scruff of his neck knocked him to the ground! This was of course during the Christmas rush, but I always got the feeling that some bus drivers seemed bent on aiming straight at you if you so much as dared to step off the kerb.

Extended Family

Providing hospitality at the centre was so demanding with the constant flow of dignitaries, missionaries and visitors from all over the world. There were always more meals to cook, sheets to wash and beds to change; in addition to meetings galore going on such as Synods, Synod Executives, special meetings and conferences. At all of these we were expected to supply endless cups of tea, coffee and refreshments. It was not unusual to have twenty- two people sit down to an evening meal in our dining room.

We tried hard to maintain a family atmosphere at meal times, so Peter, Stephen and Deborah always ate with us. With so many extra people around this put quite a strain on the children. Peter seemed to be able to cope but Stephen used to get a bit impatient with the continual stream of strangers at supper. One evening Stephen needed the sugar during the meal and politely asked several times if the sugar could be passed please. During these meals most of the VIPs got extremely engrossed in their very important conversations, and of course didn't notice Stephen's request. That was until finally Stephen seething with frustration whistled loudly and shouted at the top of his voice 'Hoy pass the sugar!' For a moment everyone was stunned and fell silent, but after the sugar was passed to the little lad, no-one seemed at all embarrassed and within seconds they were all back talking fifty to the dozen once again. Afterwards someone came to his rescue saying he had asked several times for the sugar but no-one had noticed.

On another of these occasions Bishop Ken Howell was late in arriving for supper. Stephen of course knew that we had taught him that we always said grace before meals! Fortunately there was a vacant place reserved for the Bishop at the head of the table, so he quietly slipped in, sat down and immediately began sipping his soup. Ken's arrival had not gone unnoticed however and to his great consternation Stephen suddenly bellowed at the top of his voice "Hoy, you haven't said your grace yet!" Everyone heard this time and a great silence fell upon the stunned assembly. Within seconds the slightly embarrassed Episcopal executive looked up and very contritely said "Quite right my boy, quite right!" and dutifully said his grace!

Deborah was of course much smaller, and she loved to sit on the landing upstairs on an old upturned tea chest and answer the telephone. She must have spent hours making and receiving imaginary phone calls. One day when she was about three, there were lots of guests at the meal table and Deborah was again out by the telephone. As far as we can tell there must have been a call from someone asking to speak to Bishop David Pytches. Deborah, quick as ever to answer it picked up the phone and said "Oh Bishi Pishi don't live here!" and put the receiver down again! We shall never know who that might have been. I also believe this was possibly not just a one-off, and hope our very young part time receptionist didn't cause too much confusion.

Amongst the visitors at church one Sunday evening was a dentist, who came over to speak to me. He seemed a pleasant cultured man and explained he was doing some research into indigenous people's teeth. 'Could you introduce me to some Indians, please?' he asked. I thought it was bit strange for there were several of them standing just at the side of us. 'Well here's a group here' I replied. However, as I watched him he somehow seemed scared and nervous as he glanced at them. Then seeing it was almost time to begin the service I asked him to excuse me and slipped off. At the end of the service I looked for the gentleman and asked the group 'What happened to our dentist friend?' 'Oh, he just went off without speaking to us' they replied. I later came to the conclusion that as a city dweller he'd probably never seen a Mapuche in his life and was afraid of them! Of course some Mapuches look like any other Chilean, although I had become accustomed to their features. Many of them are fairly short and stocky with rounded faces and straight black hair that tends to be a bit spiky. Others have more classical slimmer faces with long aquiline noses, like some of the indigenous Peruvian people.

It's sadly true that there was racism amongst some Chileans who had a reputation for looking down on the Mapuches. This often made it difficult for them to get jobs even when they had a good education.

We were so pleased that at least five of the lads who had been with us in the Temuco hostel later went on to university, studying electronics, law, languages and agronomy. Others became schoolteachers, carpenters and electricians. During the 1970's there were only two Mapuche members of the Chilean parliament. I later discovered that because of the racial prejudice some of those we knew actually changed their Indian names to Spanish ones.

The Mapuches generally held the missionaries in high esteem. They trusted them for their integrity far more than some of their Chilean counterparts. This was often due to the attention they received from the expatriate nurses and doctors who cared for them when they were ill. The missionary nurses also ensured they were properly attended to when going for X-rays or treatment at the government hospitals. Otherwise they were sometimes treated in an offhanded manner as if they were just uneducated country bumpkins. Many of the Mapuches also greatly benefited from the country schools founded by the Anglican missionaries in the south. Not forgetting, of course, all those who had been to the Baptist, Methodist and Roman Catholic schools and colleges.

It only rains occasionally in Santiago in the summer so I shall always remember the day it did. In fact people always removed their windscreen wipers to save them being stolen. One Sunday it actually rained during the evening service, so of course everyone came unprepared. Some asked if we could lend them umbrellas, which of course we were happy to do. Most of them on the other hand decided to wait for the rain to stop. It was our first year in the Centre and we were living on the ground floor with direct access from the church into our dining room. Normally we had our supper after the evening service once everyone had gone home. So that evening we began to get hungrier and hungrier waiting for people to leave. I don't know how many hours we waited, but by the time everyone had left it was almost bedtime! Of course, we would have been happy to invite some of them to supper, but we couldn't feed a whole church full!

Centre for Sale

When I was appointed pastor I promised the Centre congregation that I would remain there for four years. They had had a series of pastors, and had become very attached to them, but sadly none of the previous ones had stayed more than one or two years. Maybe one of the

126

reasons was that being pastor of the congregation and running the Centre was just too demanding. I now believe it was only because of an exceptional wife and the Lord's faithfulness that I was enabled to keep my promise to stay for those four years.

Soon after the coming of the Allende government the Bishop and Executive Committee felt it best to put the Centre building up for sale. The committee feared that, like so many large buildings that appeared not to be in full use, the centre would be compulsorily taken over by the government! I was therefore asked to be responsible for showing prospective buyers over the building. The major problem was because of the political situation there were very few takers. So in the interim I invited the Chilean Bible Society to use part of the ground floor as stock rooms for bibles. My greatest task followed when I had to inform the congregation that the building was for sale and we needed to look for other premises! This quite understandably stirred up a certain amount of anger amongst a few of the members. They had previously used a Methodist Church across town, but 'had been persuaded by the Mission', as one member told me, 'to move into the Centre building'. Since then they had become attached to the Centre building and it was distressing and unsettling for them to have to move once again!

Some of the missionaries, on the other hand, felt the sale of the building would resolve some of the problems concerning this multipurpose building. They argued it was a great white elephant and was never fully used, and the idea of Mission Office, Conference Centre, and church all being under one roof could never work! Another small issue was that the congregation were supposed to contribute towards the heating and lighting bills. I doubt know whether they did this on a regular basis. Even if they did they certainly saw little reason to pay for the repairs to the 'Mission building!'

So for the last few weeks before going to England I went out with the Church Council in search of alternative premises. I had a nagging feeling that perhaps some members thought it was my fault that the building was being sold! One incident was indicative of what some of our close neighbours thought about it. Whilst we were loading a lorry with pews and Church furniture, one person said. "So you are finally selling up and taking all the money back to England with you!" Florentino and Enrique were very quick to defend me, and explained that I was only the pastor and this furniture was going into store. Some pews did eventually finish up in the Renca Church, but sadly the problem of another venue for the congregation was not solved before we went on leave. Fortunately a Presbyterian Church, not too far away, did later offer the use of their building as a temporary solution.

Unbeknown to me, the biggest challenge for me yet was to come to a the farewell meal the Church members gave us. David Pytches was by this time our new Diocesan Bishop and was invited to be present. As we sat eating David came over to me and said, "John I've discovered these people love you very much, and they want me to ordain you! He went on 'So when back in England get yourself into an Anglican Theological college and I will ordain you on your return to Chile!' Previously Canon Harry Sutton had been keen for me to go Trinity College, Bristol, and be ordained but I had opted for All Nations College instead. During our time at the Centre in Santiago he, Canon Bob Smith, and Canon Ian Savile had all tried to persuade both Ann and myself about ordination, but without success. My main objection was that I was prepared to be an ordained Church leader in Chile, but certainly not in England! There was always the thought at the back of our minds that we might suddenly have to return to England because of my dad's health. Ann had also made it very clear several times that she'd married a building surveyor and didn't want to be a clergyman's wife! Now when David said the Centre congregation had appealed to him to ordain me, it seemed right and we finally agreed.

Once the Centre was sold with all its fifty-odd rooms, clearing up was a mammoth task. There were many items abandoned by numerous missionary families, much of them junk. Boxes and boxes of books, broken and discarded electrical equipment, discarded radio parts, toys, household goods, furniture and goodness knows what! As everything had to be moved out, much of it went by lorry to a large warehouse owned by the Rhab Rochette Company of which Lewis Jowett was a director. I don't remember how many lorry-loads of stuff were taken away, but Ann and I were absolutely exhausted by the end.

However, just before that we had been very pleased to welcome Canon Harry when he came to stay and enjoy hospitality with us.

Harry, it must be said, had the wonderful ability to encourage you and we were always pleased to see him. He was such a warm person, together with his wife Olive, and he would nearly always present the wives with a large box of chocolates. These were, of course, extremely expensive or non-existent at that time in Chile. Harry could see that Ann and I were by this time so tired that he urged us to return to England earlier – for I distinctly remember telling him: 'I feel like a man hanging on the edge of a cliff by my fingernails!' In other words I just didn't know how much longer I could cope. On the other hand I also felt that we were at the end of an era and the job we were doing needed to be finished – for I could not imagine anyone else doing it!

At last we moved out of the Centre some six weeks before flying home. Bishop Howell's house was now empty so we lived there in comparative luxury for the last few weeks. I knew the house quite well as I had helped Ken repair a wardrobe and other bits of their furniture. It was so sad as I remembered when he had lived there with his wife Beryl. Regrettably she had to return to England for surgery with a brain tumour. I had actually helped them pack – nailing up boxes etc – as they said their last hurried farewells to a constant flow of friends. Ken had met a brain surgeon at an Embassy event in Santiago, and this man had promised that if the Howells could return to England within two weeks he would operate immediately. Beryl's operation was fully successful, but we were all so disappointed that she only lived for about two years afterwards.

Chapter 10
LEAVE IN ENGLAND AND OAK HILL COLLEGE

On arrival back in England it was thought that a theological college in Bristol would be the best one for me. However, several of my friends from St John's Blackheath had studied at Oak Hill, and that was nearer to my parents in London I asked if I could go there. During this leave our home church very kindly offered us a lovely first-floor flat in St John's Park which belonged to it. Again the problem of the rent came up, as it had when we were last on leave, and we were again embarrassed because the Society's rent allowance just wasn't enough. Nevertheless, within a few days the situation was resolved when an anonymous benefactor from St John's came up with the difference. Members of St John's were also extremely generous in providing us with everything we needed for our home, including furniture, beds, crockery etc., although most people gave us things without fully realising that we were only back in England for about six months, and we certainly couldn't take all they had given us back to Chile.

Dr and Mrs Mumford were magnanimous in providing so many things, including an oak dining room table and six Windsor chairs. Sometimes, because people were so generous during the first few weeks there was an occasional embarrassment. For example Ruth Mumford called one Saturday morning and looking around the flat asked, "Is there anything you still need?" "Yes, we need a Telly!" piped up Stephen. "Anything else?" Ruth asked, and within half an hour she was back with a very nice portable television. Before Ruth returned I had quickly threatened Stephen that if he dare as much ask for anything else there would be dire consequences!

I enjoyed my three months at Oak Hill College and being in North London I was able to travel from home each day. Richard Lodge, then a London City Missioner, and an old friend of Boys Brigade days, very kindly lent us his Morris car to enable me to get to college and back each day. During the "Leavers' Term", as it was called, I made several friends amongst the students and found the staff extremely helpful. David Wheaton was Principal and John Taylor Vice Principal. One notable student was Cliff Richard, also there for the leavers' term, and I remember him taking part in the discussions during the ethics lectures. I discovered that he was quite shy in a crowd, but very approachable to talk to on his own.

Time passed very quickly, and I soon found I was at the end of my college course when one day I was summoned to my tutors study. We didn't know each other very well and he had the task of telling me about the plans for my future. He informed me that letters had passed between Bishop David Pytches and Canon Harry Sutton. It was now arranged that I was to be ordained by a bishop in England and then do a curacy in this country. I stood stunned and couldn't believe my ears! 'But I know nothing about these plans. Why hasn't someone told me?' I responded. My tutor seemed rather taken aback at this remark and at a loss to know what to say! Summoning up his courage, he tried to assure me that perhaps the letters sent to me had gone astray! However, I still stood there feeling rather dazed. If I remember correctly, there then followed a two minutes' silence! My voice eventually returned and I spluttered out 'But it's imperative that we return to Chile as quickly as possible. Firstly, Chile is on the brink of civil war and it will soon be impossible for foreigners to get back into the country. Secondly I'm an only child and my parents are getting used to our being in England which will make our return to Chile almost impossible!' Of course I also said that with my dad's poor health record if he became seriously ill again then I would immediately return to England. But I really needed to get back to Chile quickly! Finally I said 'Anyway I am a missionary and will always be so, and it's of secondary importance as to whether I am ordained or not!'

I later discovered this conversation caused some consternation and embarrassment at the college, not least of all to my good friend Bishop David Pytches! In no way did I want to rock the boat, but I felt it was probably almost too late to try to clarify a confused situation. The last words David had spoken to me had been to get some training and get back to Chile where he would ordain me. Looking back I am convinced the original decision was the right one. Our next most important step was to prepare to return to Chile.

Chapter 11
RETURN TO SANTIAGO AND ORDINATION

We soon packed up the flat at St John's Park, stored some small items like crockery at my mother's house, and a few boxes in my aunt Edie's spare room. Most of the furniture in the flat was left to be to be collected by its owners, except for a wardrobe and a bed that were left in the small bedroom. Friends took us by car to Dover to catch the ferry to Calais. Bill and Barbara Whitaker actually came to the quayside to say farewell, which was quite difficult as the sea was very rough and the swell was causing the vessel to rise and fall by several metres. Going down a long walkway to the ferry I happened to see a woman's passport on the floor. Looking at the photograph I was later able to find the passport's owner who was extremely grateful when I gave it to her. We then discovered she was sailing on the same passenger ship as we were and was going to Chile.

From Calais we caught an over night train passing through the outskirts of Paris during the early hours. Arriving in Genoa we found things were a bit chaotic. For some reason or other the train never reached the platform and we were forced to climb down onto the railway lines. Stumbling along as best we could to reach the platform we got there only to see the train move off with our luggage. Presenting ourselves at the luggage agent's office to complain we discovered lots of people doing the same thing. The office reassured us that our luggage would be put on board the next day when we docked in Naples. Going as quickly as we could to the quayside we were shocked to hear our names being called out on the ship's tannoy. Apparently this was the third time this announcement had been made to the Purser's great annoyance. We were puzzled and said to each other 'Surely the ship knows there is a baggage handler's strike and we've lost our luggage? It wasn't our fault we've been delayed!' Then Ann said in shear desperation 'How can we possibly travel for four weeks with three children with not even a change of clothing between us?' Then appealing to me she continued 'Surely you don't really believe the Italians will get our luggage loaded on board tomorrow?' However there was no time to discuss things; we had to get on board. The ship's sailing had already been delayed and it seemed it was partly our fault.

Again one of those depressing dark clouds was hovering over us. Yet the Lord had spoken to us that morning as we read our Bible together 'This is the day the Lord has made; let us rejoice and be glad in it!' (Psalm 118 v.24) Did God really expect us to praise Him today?

We got up early the following morning and even before breakfast there was a message from the Purser's office. We were docking in Naples and our luggage was arriving by express lorry any minute. Rushing down to the quayside I arrived before the office opened and the doors were still locked. Wonderfully the Italians had kept their promise and within minutes our luggage had arrived. Yes, we could praise the Lord once again. However this sea journey was to be a bit more eventful than previous ones.

Crisis at Sea

Half way across the Atlantic during the early hours of one morning everyone sensed the ship suddenly lurch and begin to change course. Later an announcement was made during breakfast that a Greek cargo ship had sent out a Mayday call following a fire on board. Soon after that an appeal was made for any nurses amongst the passengers to volunteer to care for those who had been badly burned. After breakfast we went up on deck to watch the ship's lifeboats being launched to go across to the distressed Greek vessel. Things started badly when an inexperienced junior officer began giving orders completely at loggerheads with those given by the ship's Bo'sun. As the lifeboats were being lowered they were swinging out and banging on the side of the ship. Heavy seas were giving our crewmen an almost impossible task as they tried to get the lifeboats into the water. The ship was rising and falling by more than ten metres. Once the boats touched the water the swell made it impossible to sail straight to the stricken vessel.

Eventually they were forced to sail in a semicircular arc. Some considerable time passed before the first batch of badly burnt sailors arrived back at the Arlanza. They were all wrapped in blankets and were quickly taken below to the ship's hospital. The volunteer nurses then worked for three exhausting days stripping the dead skin from the seriously burned sailors. I think there were at least three fatalities amongst the injured seamen. Members of our crew who had been on the rescue team reported that the Greek ship was at fault. The standard of cleanliness was very poor and piles of rubbish all over the place had ignited causing the fire! Although there were other ships in the vicinity we were the nearest to the stricken vessel that had adequate hospital facilities.

Transport Chaos

We disembarked in Valparaiso and David Pytches was there on the quayside to meet us once again. Soon it became clear that the country was in the grip of a very serious political crisis. David wanted to get us back to Santiago as soon as possible but public transport was in a state of absolute chaos. After waiting several days we were eventually allowed to travel by coach, escorted by numbers of police on motorcycles and in armed jeeps. There seemed to be about three coaches in our convoy. Electric pylons and installations were now being blown up as a regular occurrence, and "Miguelitos" (three sharp pointed nails welded together to puncture tyres) were being scattered across main roads. Even local buses had armed police guards with automatic rifles travelling up front with the driver in case of attack, which made the whole thing a bit unreal and quite frightening! The atmosphere was so tense because nobody knew what was going to happen in the end.

Within a few days of our arrival in Santiago followed a strike when most public transport and all lorries stopped running completely. Allende's government had already nationalised many industries with disastrous consequences! Nationalised bus and coach companies were already in chaos with many vehicles standing idle in their depots for lack of spares and proper servicing. This was the last straw and owners of haulage firms and lorries would not allow their businesses to go the same way.

Fortunately our luggage was transported from Valparaiso to Santiago and this gave us a chance to talk to the lorry driver. He explained that lots of the drivers owned their lorries. In fact he had been cashier in a bank and had decided to take early retirement setting himself up with his own haulage business. In no way was he going to allow the government to confiscate the lorry he bought with his own hard earned cash! During the strike a large camp was set up on the hills outside Valparaiso where drivers immobilised their vehicles to prevent them being driven off. The Chilean Navy then decided to surround the lorry park with a guard to stop anyone sabotaging the vehicles. The drivers set up camp resolved to stay with their lorries as long as was needed!

New Homes

Back safely in Santiago we had already begun house hunting, which was by now an absolutely impossible task! Many house owners were afraid to rent out their properties as the government was proposing to allow tenants the right to remain in the house with the option of buying it!

Praise God that after some time the Salvation Army came to our aid in the form of our old friend Alex Hughes. Alex made arrangements for us to borrow a very small flat over their bookshop in the street called Augustinas. I think it had one bedroom, a living room and a tiny kitchen. We were, to say the least, so relieved and grateful to God – and of course the kindness of the Salvation Army! During the following weeks Peter and Stephen were intrigued to hear the Salvation Army band regularly playing in the Citadel next door. On Sunday afternoons they would go to the service just to hear the band play. Thus began their enthusiasm for brass bands. Later they both joined their school brass band in Harrow, and eventually the Kirkby Miners Welfare Band when we moved up to Nottinghamshire.

Our house in Las Carretas Street, Santiago

From the flat over the bookshop we moved to the northern side of Santiago to a street called Las Carretas. This was a modern bungalow in a residential area belonging to the American Baptist Church. Our

136

landlords were very scared of the government's new legislation and were really pleased to get some friendly tenants! This was to be our first experience of living in a residential area amongst professional people. While we lived there the boys and later Deborah had some very enjoyable days at Santiago Academy. The school was quite small with only two or three very dedicated American teachers. Although the lessons were taught in English the children preferred speaking Spanish in their free time or playing together.

Ordained

As soon as I got the opportunity I raised the question of ordination with Bishop David Pytches. He explained that my refusal to do a curacy in England had caused him quite a problem. David had not expected me to be back in Chile so soon; he had intended me to do a curacy in England first!

So David finally decided to ordain me not in Santiago but outside the region in Viña del Mar. Prior to this I was to have a retreat in David's house, during which time the Rev Tony Valencia was nominated to examine me on Infant Baptism! Not a subject I would have chosen myself, but I suppose I must have given the right sort of answers according to my theological reading.

I was made deacon in the Quilpue Church, which was the house where Brian and Gill Skinner lived and where Brian was the Pastor. The Service was simple, quite informal, but for me very moving. It was part of a quiet day held for the missionaries who were the main members of the congregation. The most significant part for me was when David asked Ann and I to kneel side by side together and then placed his hands on us both. For me this was so symbolic as we had agreed to serve the Lord together, wherever that might be in the future, before we got married. We have an inscription in both our wedding rings which says 'Glorify the Lord with me and let us exalt his name together.' (Psalm 34 v.3). We had chosen these words because Jim Elliot and his wife Elizabeth had these verses engraved in their wedding rings. Later Jim Elliot with four companions was killed by Auca Indians in Ecuador. He is still a constant challenge to me personally.

On Sunday 7th October 1972, in the Church of San Pedro Viña del Mar, I was ordained 'Presbitero'. During the service our friend Anthony Smyth preached appropriately from the verse 'Watch your life and your teaching closely' (I Timothy 4 v.16)

Ordination 7th October 1972.
San Pedro Church,
Vina del Mar.

The word 'Presbitero' is Spanish for Presbyter and is extremely important to me as I find the word 'Priest' in the Prayer Book tends to confuse people. In the New Testament the word priest is the name given to all Christians. Peter says all Christians are 'a chosen people, a royal priesthood'. (I Peter chapter 2 verses 4 and 9). The Christian priesthood has nothing to do with the priests of the Old Testament. Our priesthood means we are chosen to have access to God and can approach Him at any time. The sacrifices we offer are spiritual ones such as our work, our worship and ourselves. Every Christian is also chosen to declare God's praises for 'calling us out of darkness into His wonderful light' and for Jesus' sacrificial death on the cross for our sins.

After ordination we returned to the bungalow in Santiago in the street called Las Carretas. Our neighbours next door were very friendly and easy to get on with. Conditions under the Allende government just continued to get worse and worse and shortages of food were our biggest problem. Consequently whenever anything arrived at our corner shop, like margarine or cake mixtures, our neighbour's children came across to let us know and we would rush up to the shop! One day coming home I saw a queue outside. I asked a lady what she was hoping to buy and as she didn't seem to know I joined the queue anyway. At last each person was coming away with a bottle; we were queuing for Whisky! People were quite surprised when I turned away, but there was nothing on the shelves, for apart from matches the shop was completely empty of anything! Of course some people would swap what they didn't want for something they did, and we soon began to learn to do that too!

Several Good Turns Deserve a Volkswagen!

One afternoon I had a phone call from our friend Alex Hughes saying could I possibly help? He had of course been extremely helpful in making the Salvation Army flat available to us, so here was a chance to help him in return. Their band was about to go on tour, but the tyres on their lorry were worn out and they couldn't get new ones. The political situation meant that tyres and car spares were completely unavailable. 'Could I possibly lend them the Mission Volkswagen?' Alex asked me. They would only be away for 10 days, and feeling their need was greater than mine I agreed! They drove the vehicle off and I didn't expect to hear any more assuming they were on tour down South somewhere.

Horror of horrors a few days later as they were getting near to Concepcion the vehicle suffered a major breakdown! Klaus, Alex's brother in law, rang saying a piston rod had punched a hole through one of the pistons! Managing to get the car towed to a Volkswagen garage the owner had then given them a gigantic repair bill! I talked to him on the telephone but failed to get him to reduce the cost. Feeling desperate, and rather playing for time, I asked if he could possibly send me a detailed estimate. Showing this to Sheila Baughan she said there just wasn't that amount of money for a repair bill of that enormity! I then found myself in an even worse situation. Eventually ringing the garage owner I explained we had no money to repair the vehicle and I was expected to bring it back to Santiago.

After a long tedious journey Ray Smith and I arrived at the garage to find the owner was at lunch. When he did appear we found him already in a very bad mood. Unfortunately two of his mechanics had taken out a customer's car on test and had smashed it up! He asked me if the vehicle had been used for ploughing, as the engine was full of earth! Reluctantly he led me through to the workshop to inspect the engine. I was however completely unprepared for what I would see as before me was the engine spread out like a sea of car spares, down to the smallest nut and bolt! He was absolutely fuming and finally announced 'So you want to take the vehicle away. Well you can go through all these parts, and check they are all here.' Having eventually done that he finally produced several sheets of paper and demanded that I sign for them!

I was feeling mentally battered, but Ray Smith had been waiting very patiently whilst all this was going on. Once every one of the pieces had been loaded onto the vehicle we could get going, with Ray towing the disabled vehicle. It was now late in the afternoon before we eventually began our return journey to Santiago. But we were not out of the wood yet for before getting half way home we were forced to abandon the vehicle at the roadside. The lights were not working and we dare not risk being hit by a lorry during the darkness. I felt very unhappy about abandoning the vehicle on a country road intending to come back for it the next day. This was Chile and I was convinced that in the mean time the wheels would be stripped off, or maybe the vehicle would be stolen! Praise the Lord my worst fears were wrong, the vehicle was safe, and we arrived back in Santiago plus the engine all in pieces the next day!

Once home, despite any faint hopes I may have had, there was no possible way of getting the vehicle repaired. It just had to sadly stand on our forecourt outside the bungalow for the next ten months! With the political crisis continuing it was just impossible to import new pistons. Speaking to David Pytches he asked 'why on earth did you lend the vehicle to the Salvation Army anyway?' I tried to explain that although I was reluctant to do so I felt I should help them as they had helped us on several occasions.

The final outcome came many months later when Alex rang me suggesting I contact the garage where they had the Salvation Army vehicles repaired. The manager was very helpful and made it clear that whilst they still could not get new spares, he had some second hand pistons. He could repair the car and although the engine would not have the same power as before at least it would be operational. So we asked the garage to carry out the work and the Volkswagen was once again back on the road!

Although having got myself into serious trouble this didn't cancel out my sense of gratitude to Alex who had helped us on several occasions. The one I most vividly remember was when I was Pastor of the Centre congregation. We wanted to organise a treat for the children from the shantytown Sunday Schools. Alex said if we could pay for the petrol he would borrow a Salvation Army lorry on his day off and collect all the children and then take them home afterwards. An extra bonus on that day was that Alex also brought his concertina and led the children in singing whilst we organised games and refreshments. Several helpers made up the team that day including Thea Coates, Zoila Pranao and Raúl from the Centre congregation.

For the shantytown children to have such an outing in the O'Higgins Park was probably one of the most memorable days of their lives.

All went smoothly that day much to my surprise. The biggest problem came when it was time to go home. The children just refused to get back on the lorry! As fast as we got some on board others jumped off. Even the ones who had been bathing in an ornamental pond (which was full of old iron bedsteads and bits of bicycles) came out and then jumped back in again! Park keepers ordered them to come out but they took no notice! I was at my wits end when suddenly the Lord came to my rescue with an idea! Across the park I saw an ice cream man slowly pushing the peddles on his old fashioned tricycle. Ignoring the expense I sped over to ask if he could possibly supply seventy ice creams. Returning to the children I then promised that everyone would get an ice cream once they were on the lorry. The Sunday school teachers and other helpers marshalled the youngsters into lines. Standing on the lorry I then handed each one an ice cream once they had climbed on board! At last Alex was then able to drive around Santiago dropping the children off at their different shantytowns and housing estates.

Home Truths

However, I must continue about our new home in a residential area of Santiago. Our neighbours next door were a retired couple with two or three grown up children. Mr Naranjo had worked as an industrial chemist in the copper mines in Rancagua. Their youngest daughter was still at home and studying at dental school. Because of the seriousness of the political situation Mr Naranjo and others decided to set up a neighbourhood watch. Meetings were normally held in the Naranjo's house to inform and advise us on the growing crisis. It was suggested that we try to stock up on paraffin, and possibly keep several large drums stored in the garden. I thought this could be illegal and could be a fire hazard, so I decided against it. We never used paraffin, although many poorer people did for heating and cooking. On the other hand I suppose it might have been useful in the latter days of the Allende regime. During those days electricity was often cut off because installations were blown up or sabotaged.

Many people were convinced things were going to finish up with civil war. At our neighbourhood watch meeting we were advised that in case of street fighting, with shooting in the streets, we should put

Changing the guard at the Moneda Palace

mattresses up at the windows and lay down on the floor. In the mean time they organised nightly patrol when the men walked the streets in twos, armed with a revolver or shotgun! I explained to Mr Naranjo that as I was a Pastor I couldn't carry arms; he just said not to worry I could accompany him! So I went out several evenings with him and we chatted together. He said he was appalled at what the government was doing, as were so many other professional people. The opposition was also partly to blame as there were so many rumours and counter rumours that you didn't know what to believe. Certainly the government was no longer in control and no one could guess what was going to happen.

One lunchtime Mr Naranjo's daughter was driving up a one-way street on the way home from dental school. Suddenly, utterly amazed, she was confronted by a cortege of black Limousines coming towards her! The President was returning to his office in the Moneda Palace after going home for lunch. Amongst the men in the cars was his bodyguard called the GAP "Groupo de Amigos del Presidente." As they forced the young student's car over she was so outraged that winding down the window she screamed "You son of a bitch!" (or probably some similar expletive in Spanish) as the President's car swept past!

142

Enigmatic President, Polarized Nation

When Allende became President it was his last chance, having stood twice before and not been elected. He scraped in by a narrow margin of a few hundred votes, which meant that he needed the approval of Congress to take office. Once in office so much of the new legislation he forced through was done by decree and not by act of parliament. Later during governmental elections many believed there had been considerable vote rigging. Certainly whole sacks full of voting papers were found dumped in the river Mapocho. Several national newspapers also alleged that many ballot papers had been filled in by people who had been dead for years! Great unrest was growing at the way the country was going. On two or three occasions Allende announced publicly over the media that people were plotting to assassinate him. I'm sure this was true and he actually declared on the media that he knew their names.

His regime caused an enormous amount of hatred to be engendered, and I used to attend regular meetings with Christians from different denominations to pray for peace. Frequently groups of Christians would go out before daybreak and paste stickers along the kerbs in the centre of the city with the words "Love not Hate". The whole country was being polarized into two camps, one on the right and the other on the left. A vicious class war was being engendered where workers and employers were made to feel they were on opposing sides. Many working farms were taken over by the workers, whilst the authorities were always conspicuous by their absence. The police did nothing to protect defenceless owners when gangs turned up to evict them. Often farm owners were forced to leave heir homes with just a few clothes, some not even being allowed to take their cars! I have actually watched people painting pro-government graffiti, being guarded by police to stop any interference. Graffiti was fairly common but nevertheless it was still illegal!

Queues and Shortages

Food was becoming so short that the average family was spending up to six hours queuing every day! Some people gave up work to queue as a full time occupation selling their purchases to others. People who employed a maid would mostly send them out to do the queuing. A growing black market was offering petrol at three to five times the price. Later when working in the hospital a friend gave me a phone number saying "Just say you want some carnations and you will get meat delivered to your door!" One day I met a man riding an old tricycle, like the ones that we used to see selling ice creams when I was a child. Seeing he was loaded with bread I crossed the road and approached him saying "Could I buy a couple of loaves please?" Looking at me a bit quizzically he shook his head and replied "It's only for those who have a card!" He didn't say what card, but I then realized this was part of the President's "Popular Basket" policy. The scheme was for the benefit of people living in the shantytowns where parcels of groceries including bread, butter, and a chicken were regularly delivered. Part of the irony was that most poor people never ate butter anyway!

One Saturday Ann and I queued at a large supermarket for nearly four hours. Getting to the entrance we found most things had finished except for a bag of sugar and a packet of washing powder! We met regularly for prayer with others and before going home we would spend time swapping things for items of food. Our children were now getting fed up with porridge as it often contained weevils, with moths in the flour, because the packets had been stored so long! Bread was in very short supply, so sometimes we bought packets of cake mixture, until they eventually ran out as well! Later when working in the hospital the dieticians encouraged me ask for stale bread from the kitchens to take home. This would normally be thrown away so if I got some Ann soaked it in water and put in the oven, but I was too embarrassed to ask very often.

On some Sunday mornings I would visit the family of Church members. One day Luis was at work but his wife was at home. Opening the door the lovely smell of newly baked bread wafted up from the kitchen. Later as I was leaving she went through to the kitchen to return and hand me a warm freshly baked loaf of bread saying "Take this home to your wife and children; I know you must be short of bread!" She had just enough flour for two loaves and gave me one! At this stage no one had seen a loaf of bread in the shops for six weeks! We had tried to supplement our meagre diet by stocking up on packets of dried beans, lentils and dried fruit.

Chapter 12
HOSPITAL CHAPLAINCY

Things were still getting worse every day when Alberto Kuppfer contacted me. When we were working in the Centre he had asked me to join him as part of the Chaplains team to a group of five hospitals. I had refused saying I hadn't got time – in reality I just didn't want to do that sort of thing! That had been a year ago, and now although ordained, ironically I found myself without a Church! During our absence in England the missionaries used to meet each week for prayer. At one of these meetings it was unanimously decided that I should work in the Hospital with Alberto! I was still extremely reluctant and quite put out that things had been decided without me even being consulted! Later, however with hindsight, this was obviously the Lord's will for me! So I went down to meet Alberto in his office at the old Infirmary.

Alberto was a very committed Christian with an extremely active and intelligent mind. He came from a fairly well off family and when he was struck with blindness he travelled to Switzerland to see a senior eye surgeon. After extensive tests the man told Alberto that if he insisted he could operate. However there could be no assurance that the operation would be successful and there was a high risk that the

Pentecostals visiting the Infirmary

pupils could disintegrate! Alberto philosophically told me that the Lord had allowed him to remain blind to keep him humble. 'Otherwise it would be impossible to live with me because of my intelligence,' he added. He not only spoke fluent Spanish, but also had a good command of English and his first language was German. His father had been Swiss Consul in Santiago. Alberto was Pastor of a Church called 'The Church of the

Lord', one of the many branches of the Pentecostal Church in Chile. The members of his Santiago congregation came mainly from professional families, and included nurses, medical and other students.

Alberto told me the story of how he came to be the first paid Protestant Chaplain in the Chilean National Health Service. His aged mother had to be taken into the geriatric part of the old Infirmary in Santiago and he visited her regularly on Sundays with his wife Trudi. Walking through the long wards in the old hospital he soon came to realise that the patients hardly ever had any visitors. He was distressed by this and decided to contact the Director of the Hospital Group to request that a Chaplain be appointed. The Director invited him to his office and listened intently to him. 'Now I want to take fourteen days to talk to pastors in the city and invite them to apply to be interviewed for the Protestant Chaplain's post,' were his closing remarks. Alberto was soon very discouraged to find that not one of them was prepared to even consider it! So in less than the fourteen days he returned to the Director to tell him of the complete lack of response. With great disappointment Alberto reported back to the Director who replied "Well, look here I give you the position!" Immediately responding with utter disbelief Albert said "But I am completely blind how could I do it?" To which the Director replied "Oh well, in fact I suffer from bad eyesight myself, take the job – when can you start?" Arrangements were then made for Alberto to receive a small salary as a clerical assistant, although in fact he had no such duties, and everyone knew he was a Pastor, working as Protestant Chaplain!

Within a short space of time Alberto came to be greatly appreciated and respected. Up until that time the only chaplains in any hospital had been Roman Catholic Priests. Alberto fortunately had a small private income, as formerly he had worked as Sales Director in his father's foundry. Becoming blind in is early forties was an enormous blow to him, for he had been a keen sportsman and especially enjoyed horse riding. It was obvious he was a trained engineer from his conversation. Very occasionally when I gave him a lift in the mission vehicle, he would comment that something was wrong by the sound of the engine, or the fan belt was loose or whatever! He scared me stiff one afternoon when I was giving him a lift as the vehicle stalled and he immediately jumped out. At once walking round to the back he began pushing, and left himself standing alone in the middle of a busy road as the vehicle started! Putting on the hazard lights, I quickly stopped the vehicle and got him back inside. Alberto actually owned the taxi that brought him to work, and he normally telephoned his driver during the day if he needed to go somewhere in the city.

Sometimes Alberto and I would walk along the corridors together in the El Salvador hospital. He knew the place like the back of his hand and could correct me if I went the wrong way. Normally though he had a member of his congregation to act as guide for him walking along holding their arm. In the hospital corridors people would frequently greet him, and recognising their voice he would nearly always answer them using their first names. He not only recognised a person by their voice; he would know how they were by the tone of their voice! Also as he shook their hands, or place a hand on their shoulders, he would sense that they were tense or tired and comment on it. Members of staff would share their problems with him. As I was walking with him one day a medical secretary began talking to him at length about her mother. The old lady was becoming senile and living on her own was of great concern to the daughter. Suddenly looking at me she said "Oh I shouldn't have said all that," and became very embarrassed. Wishing to put her at ease I said 'Oh I'll not repeat a word, Alberto can't see and I can't hear!" We all laughed and she felt a bit better!

Padre Joseph, one of the two Roman Catholic Chaplains, was an American in his early seventies and had served faithfully in the Hospital as Chaplain for twenty-two years. He was a very compassionate man and helped me a lot and was always at hand to give me advice. On our return journey to England Padre Joseph actually arranged for us to meet him in Chicago, and took all our family out for an expensive meal in a restaurant called Louis Berkoff's. I don't think Peter and Stephen had ever been in such a posh restaurant. Looking down the table Padre Joseph said 'Now boys you just order whatever you like and you can have it!' I don't ever remember saying that to them, so they both looked at me in utter bewilderment and said 'Is that right Dad?' Afterwards Padre Joseph took us into a large Woolworths and bought all the children toys. He was a wonderful man. Later I sadly discovered he had returned to the States to live near his sister as he was ill and died of cancer.

The other Roman Catholic Chaplain was Padre Aldo who was Italian and had been ordained in a wheel chair in Italy to work amongst disabled people. He suffered from an incurable kidney disease which meant each month he would have to stay in bed for three days with a high fever. He was becoming weaker all the time and had difficulty with writing and wore braces to strengthen his wrists. Aldo worked tirelessly in the hospital and outside setting up several houses for disabled people in and around Santiago. On Fridays he was not in the hospital as he was attending to the needs of these people in these centres.

Chaplaincy amid Political Chaos

The three chaplains were such an example and challenge to me as I realised I was the youngest and most able-bodied one amongst them. I really admired their commitment. I still sometimes wonder exactly why the Lord chose me to do this work in the hospital. Although after the military seized power I was just in the right place to help so many needy and distressed people and political prisoners.

Both Joseph and Aldo were very gifted with children, and the children loved them. Alberto and I found we got on extremely well with them both and we all four had breakfast together on Tuesdays. Joseph often came out with some conundrum or trick that he had used with children. After breakfast we normally talked about different patients and then prayed together.

Catholics and Protestants were working well together despite all the political upheaval and there were regular joint meetings praying for renewal in the Churches in Santiago. Sometimes on Tuesday mornings walking past the Hospital Chapel I would hear the nuns singing as they played their guitars and led the Service. I also met others working on the wards, dressed of course in their nurse's uniforms. All were highly praised by the patients for their excellence in nursing skills, care, and dedication!

Just before the Coup d'état a young Chilean Priest, whom I met out of town in a queue for petrol, invited me to preach at Mass. I was really looking forward to this but sadly in the end I was bitterly disappointed. Arriving at the hospital that morning I found myself in the middle of a large political demonstration! Consequently I was so delayed that by the time I got to the chapel the service had finished!

That morning the whole hospital was in chaos, with so much commotion and parts of the hospital sealed off. Going down to the basement to see the head dietician I found a distressed dietician. She was a young mum who had witnessed the demonstration by the Central Pharmacy. Taking her small daughter to the nursery she found herself in the centre of shooting, with bullets bouncing off the floor between her legs! She was so scared that scooping up her small daughter she quickly ran to the basement to a place of safely!

Strikes by hospital staff were the order of the day at this time, plus interminable meetings in the lecture rooms during hospital time. Because of this I would often find all the nurses, auxiliaries and porters were out of sight with no one on the wards. Even worse was that the people at these meetings were never able to make any decisions. They had never had that responsibility before. So after spending hours discussing matters the meetings were always a terrible waste of time.

This state of affairs was being repeated again and again in work places throughout the country. For example the plastics industry had previously been very successful both at home and exporting abroad. Now it was in chaos, with damage being done to the machinery and explosions happening, because the operatives didn't know what they were doing. A neighbour of ours across the road, who taught agronomy in the university, said to me one day 'Would you let a gardener repair your television, well I certainly wouldn't!'

Luis one of our Church members was a supervisor in a famous cooked meat factory. The Popular Unity government had decided that they would no longer employ food inspectors in the factory as the workers could do the inspections themselves. Luis said that at the end of every afternoon the routine had been to wash the machines down with boiling water ready for the following day. Now under the new order this was no longer being done so particles of rotting meat and maggots were being found in the machines in the morning. Luis was a very conscientious person who had worked in the company for many years. He was becoming completely disillusioned with the way the factory was now being run.

We were living in an absolutely chaotic period. In the hospitals there were shortages of drugs, needles, cotton wool, cleaning materials, sheets and theatre linen and all sorts of supplies. Often patients needing major surgery having travelled hundreds of miles to get to Santiago were sent back home again.

Alberto had previously received supplies of dried milk and vitamins from the United States. This he distributed to the poorer people as they arrived at the out-patients clinics. Patients had to get to hospital very early in the morning and then wait three or four hours before seeing a doctor. It had always been distressing to see the young mothers with their babies sitting on the hard wooden benches in the corridors. Many were maids who had asked for time off from work. Some having waited the whole morning would then be told to come back the following day. Several had been known to faint on arrival after having left home at such an early hour without breakfast!

After some months members of staff in the hospital began to get to know me. One day as I was walking past the central stores one of the store men greeted me. "How are you fixed for powdered milk and vitamins these days?' he asked. Then continuing he added "If you need any for those young mums just ask me and I'll blow the doors off the main store for you!" He said this with a large facetious grin! He was member of an extreme group called the MIR (Revolutionary Movement of the Left) so I made it quite clear that in no way could I accept that sort of offer! Although he had spoken with typical Chilean humour I knew he wasn't joking!

I usually worked in the hospital on Tuesdays, Thursdays and Fridays, and was allowed to eat in the refectory at lunchtime. During lunch one day I found myself sitting near to one of Alberto's brothers who was a doctor. The whole family were extremely gifted and this brother, like Alberto, was also completely blind, but this one was a confirmed atheist.

Interestingly I was never expected to wear a clerical collar, but I did have to wear a white coat with a Hospital Chaplain's armband. The two hospitals I mainly worked in were the Chest Hospital (350 beds), and the Lopez Perez Cancer Foundation (about 70 beds). In addition I was sometimes asked to visit the El Salvador hospital where there were medical and surgical wards, plus a maternity wing. There was also a Neuro-logical Hospital and an

Infirmary for old people. All these hospitals were on the same campus with a total of between 2000 and 2500 beds, so there was always more visiting than we could cope with. At times Alberto would ask me to attend meetings on his behalf. I found these very taxing and tried hard to lip read, but still found it difficult to understand what people were saying. Although the lady Director was very kind and was always glad that I actually came. Later I excused myself from meetings as these took up so much time and I felt my priority should be to be on the wards visiting the patients. I also

 declined to be on the Social committee and told Cristina, the head dietician, that they were much better at organising things than I was. Alberto on the other hand was incred-ible and would attend so many meetings, relate the important points raised, and tell me how they were to be implemented.

Chest Hospital,
Santiago

More Lessons from the Pentecostals

After lunch on Tuesdays I had to co-ordinate a short service in the small chapel in the Infirmary. This was attended by about anything up to 30 ladies from different Pentecostal Churches who would afterwards then go on to visit the wards. On one occasion they told me of a young Baptist Pastor who was seriously ill with kidney failure and awaiting surgery. Today, of course, he would have needed a kidney transplant. We prayed for healing but we knew we were asking for a big miracle. Unfortunately the operation never happened. But the volunteers continued to pray for the Pastor who had a young family. One afternoon the ladies informed me that they were going to visit the sick Pastor. We prayed beforehand, and I asked that no more than a couple of them visit him, as he was so weak.

151

The ladies had such a motherly concern for him and assured me they would only stay a few minutes. As I had to pass the ward later I thought I would just look in. To my amazement and considerable concern there were eight ladies around the bed, all talking a great deal, and even asking the poor man to pray for them! I gently but firmly got them to leave. Sadly within two days the Pastor died.

A group of forty men from the Pentecostal Churches would visit the infirmary on Sunday mornings. At 10.00 am they held a service in the Chapel and then processed playing their guitars and singing through the hospital grounds. Several of these men had been incredibly healed and sometimes I would be in tears as I listened to their testimonies. Not stopping for food they spent many hours on the wards laying hands on the sick and praying for them, eventually returning to their Church for tea before the evening service. These Pentecostal Christians taught me so much about commitment, faithfulness, and the ministry of all believers. They also greatly supplemented the work of the chaplains as there were always more patients to visit than we could manage.

Of course some of the doctors were a bit cynical and one senior medic said to me vehemently "these Pentecostals are not coming onto my patch as they cause absolute havoc!" Yet another doctor confided in me that he was happy to allow them access to his department, 'because of the encouragement and comfort they bring to the patients – especially those who never receive any visitors'.

Pentecostal Christians were never allowed to visit the cancer patients. In fact one senior sister told me that visiting hours were always traumatic anyway. Visitors sat around the beds ignoring the patients, animatedly talking to each other, preoccupied with their own problems and personal anxieties. Consequently when visiting time was over patients could be distressed, distraught and frequently in tears. It was not surprising therefore that staff were glad when visiting hours ended so that they could then begin to try to calm and comfort the patients.

Orange Juice Opens the Door

I was learning quite a bit about pastoral care, the problems and the need for sensitivity when visiting people who are ill. Working in the hospital the Lord taught me so much and I saw Him do great things with both patients and staff. That is to say not all the sick were healed. Some were, others were changed, and still others came to know Jesus in a real and personal way.

One day I went to visit a man with a bullet lodged in his lungs. He had shot and killed a policeman and had been brought from prison to the Chest hospital for treatment. He had two armed prison guards at the entrance to the ward that gave a bit of an ominous feeling. The patient was like a skeleton, unshaven with several days of growth of beard, and was extremely weak! At first he refused to speak to me! Yet I felt it was important I continue to visit him and pray for him a lot in between visits. Being fairly practical the Lord gave me the idea that perhaps some oranges, crushed to make him a drink, might be a way to get through to him. So I spoke to the male nurse and he said that would be in order, and he was happy to make the drink. Oranges of course grow in Chile, and pure orange juice is a favourite drink. So knowing Thea Coates had a tree in the garden I asked her permission to pick some.

The next time I visited the man he thanked me for the orange juice. At last he began to talk to me – he was an extremist rather than a criminal. His family had disowned him and his girl friend had left him. Sadly it was later found impossible to remove the bullet and after several weeks the man was returned to prison. Before that he did allow me to pray with him – and one day I was able to explain that Jesus had died for him and loved him very much. He gave his life to Christ and after that we had a good relationship.

On the stairs one day the Director of the hospital said to me "Your patient is getting better!" I remember then saying to her 'two armed guards with automatic rifles standing at the ward entrance is not conducive to his healing! He is after all not going to escape; he's too weak to even stand up! Why can't the prison officers wear white coats to look like hospital staff?' Nevertheless some days later I was disappointed to discover he had been taken from the hospital and we had not been able to say farewell. Sadly I was never able to get any more details about him from the hospital and I never saw him again.

Ministry with the Social Workers
Tuesday afternoons, following the short service in the chapel, I would call at the social workers office to see if there were any referrals for

me. Arriving one afternoon Magali said 'Ah you're just the person we want to see, this lady here is a believer!' The lady was seated in the middle of the office slumped forward and sobbing her heart out. I squatted down beside her, and asked her several times to please stop crying and tell me what was wrong. Eventually she said that she suffered from tuberculosis and had come for a check up that morning. To her great distress the doctor told her she was much worse than he anticipated and she needed to be hospitalised. Several things were worrying her, although none in fact were to do with her medical condition! The children would come home from school and not know where she was. Her husband would come home from work and there would be no meal ready for him. And lastly she hadn't got any toiletries i.e. - not even a toothbrush or bar of soap – let alone a nightdress! She mentioned about five things and began to cry again.

"How can I help her Lord?" I prayed quietly in my heart. Then some words of St Paul came to my mind - "Do not be anxious about anything, but in everything, by prayer and petition, with thanksgiving let your requests be made known to God, and the peace of God that passes all understanding will keep your hearts and your minds in Christ Jesus". (Philippians Chapter 4 verses 6,7.) Fortunately I was able to repeat these verses from memory and she seemed to be familiar with them. So I then said 'What I want you to do is get a piece of paper and write down a list of these needs and start praying.' Promising I would see her in two days time I left the office. Thursday afternoon came and I called into the ward where she was. It was only a small one and she turned her head to smile at me! 'How are things?' I asked. 'Well the Lord has answered three of my requests and there's just two to go!' she replied.

Over a period of time I got to know two of the Social Workers very well. Magali had just returned to work after being off sick for many months due to a nervous breakdown. She told me months had gone by but things didn't really improve, she went out for long walks, went to occasional social events and concerts, but nothing changed. Then one day the specialist said to her "The thing you need is to get yourself a good religion!" I made no comment at the time she related this to me. The wonderful surprise was to come many months later. For one afternoon Magali amazed me by saying that she had become a Christian after watching the way the Lord had worked in the lives of patients I had talked to and prayed with! In fact she had listened carefully to my conversation with the lady who had been crying in the office that day. Magali had then made her own list of requests, and the Lord had answered her prayers as well! I found this both astonishing and very humbling for I had no idea she had been observing things so closely!

After becoming a Christian Magali then came with her husband Eduardo and Norma, another Social Worker, plus a few hospital staff to a small Bible study in our house. The time was soon drawing near when we should be returning to England. However right until a few weeks before that I had no idea who would take over as chaplain after me. After praying about it I asked Magali if in the future she might like some tracts to give to patients. With a radiant smile she beamed 'do you mean you are asking me to take over some of the work you've been doing, I would really consider that to be a great privilege!'

One Tuesday afternoon I arrived to find that Magali and Norma were both out of the office. But there was another Social Worker whom I had never met before, and I noticed how very strained and stressed she looked. When I asked how she was and she replied she had a very bad headache and was extremely concerned about her son. Continuing she said 'I think he is hoping to get to France because he is wanted by the authorities!' 'Would you like me to pray for you?' I asked. 'No I'm an atheist' she retorted abruptly. 'Don't you think the Lord can heal atheists then?' I asked. Then without further ado I just bowed my head and prayed for her. After a few seconds looking up I asked her "How are you feeling now?" She replied that she was extremely embarrassed because she was already feeling a bit better!

Fridays and Healings
On Friday afternoons I usually visited the 'Lopez Perez' cancer Foundation. At that time this was the only NHS hospital where patients could receive radiotherapy. Patients would often come hundreds of miles and had to stay in a large house in the hospital grounds until a hospital bed became available. The Lopez Perez also carried out quite a lot of major surgery and had some very dedicated nurses and doctors. One of these doctors would call me into his office to discuss ethical matters with him. He said plainly he had no truck with the Roman Catholic Priests and preferred to ask my opinion on matters. Later when he himself was a patient in hospital I

was able to visit him and he seemed encouraged by our conversation. He even corrected some of my Spanish.

One afternoon entering a cancer ward, dressed in my white coat, there was a visitor sitting at the side of a patient. At once, without getting a chance to introduce myself, the patient suddenly pulled her nightdress right up and bared everything! Rather taken aback I blinked, and then stammered that actually I had come to examine her soul not her body! The visitor who was a Christian then told me how her sister was very ill adding "I am praying she will come to know the Lord before she dies!" The following week I didn't see the patient as she had returned home. So having her address I called at her flat, and getting no answer I wrote on a tract and slipped it under the door. Six weeks passed and then I received a letter from the sister who lived in Valparaiso. Her dear sister had died but she was so grateful that she had come to know the Lord beforehand!

Another Friday I met a very distressed old lady in her early eighties. She had travelled a long journey by air needing an operation to remove a tumour. She was so miserable because to remove the tumour they had to take out her eye! 'I've lived all these years and now at my age I have to lose my eye! Surely they could do it some other way!' she told me with some anguish. I just didn't know how to comfort her so I said I would ask another Chaplain to visit her. Later I explained all about her to Alberto and asked him to visit her. After the weekend I went back to see her. 'How did you get on with the other Chaplain?' I asked. She exclaimed 'Well he first felt for the bottom rail of the bed with his hands. Then looking in my direction he asked me "how many eyes did you say you have got to have removed?" The old lady then of course realised that Alberto was totally blind and was lost for words. Later she confessed to me that perhaps she was making a bit too much fuss!

Padre Aldo was never in the hospital on Friday as he was usually visiting his homes for handicapped people. One afternoon neither Padre Joseph nor Padre Aldo were available, and walking into a small ward I found myself talking to the Headmistress of a Roman Catholic School. She was a Nun and had breast cancer and so much wanted to take Holy Communion. We talked for a bit and realised that we should both get into trouble if I gave her Communion. Finally I said 'Well the thing I can do is to pray with you!' and I prayed with her. I never saw her again but discovered many months later that she had been healed! It happened that I was invited to speak at St Andrews English Church about the Hospital Chaplaincy work. As I listened to the person introducing me I suddenly realised he was speaking about the incident concerning the nun's healing! But I was even more astonished when he actually repeated the words of my prayer - which had been extemporary – and which I certainly couldn't remember! All I could do was to give glory to God! Isn't it fantastic when God answers our prayers when we've forgotten all about them! Yet that's the way the Lord works sometimes. So there's no room for pride, just humble praise!

Just before breakfast one morning, when I was getting ready to leave for the hospital, a neighbour came across from a house opposite. Her small niece had been knocked down by a taxi and was in the Neurological Hospital – could we pray for her? I decided I would see the little girl that morning as she was in the neurology part of the El Salvador hospital. I don't remember her name but she was eight and I asked a staff nurse how she was? She replied no one would know yet as it was a matter of wait and see – it could be weeks! Consequently each day I called to see the little girl, and placing my hands on her cot rail prayed for her. There was never any change she just continued to be unconscious. Eight weeks passed until one morning, putting my head round the Sister's office door, I asked 'How is the little girl please?' 'She's all right.' came the reply. Puzzled I asked the nurse what that meant. She just repeated what she had said. 'Was there any brain damage or anything?' I ventured. 'No there doesn't seem to be!' came the brief reply. I was overcome with joy – I would rush in to see her. But then I paused - for the little girl didn't know me - she had never seen me before! So entering the ward and smiling I just said 'Hello!' She just looked up at me rather wide-eyed, but as she said nothing I decided to slip away! Returning home later that day I just rushed to the study and dropping to my knees praised God with tears trickling down my cheeks.

Of course there were times when people were not healed. And generally the policy in the hospitals was to send people home to die. Going into one ward I got chatting to a man with cancer. It turned out that he lived just across the road from the Church at Renca. He was drummer in a band, working at night in a restaurant always getting home in the early hours of the morning. He knew he hadn't long to live and one afternoon he showed me lots of photographs of himself playing in the band. He told me he had a dedicated wife and several daughters but his great sadness was that he had never had a son. Then to my surprise he told me his wife was pregnant and expecting a baby any day. 'Perhaps we should pray for your wife to have a baby son?' I suggested. He was a bit sceptical, saying 'well I prayed that God would heal me, but that prayer has not been answered.' Anyway we prayed together before I left. A few days later I was called by the ward to discover that they were getting him ready to go home. I asked permission to travel with him in the ambulance and we arrived at his house in Renca. His wife and children were so pleased to see him - and to our great surprise the baby had arrived – and it was a boy! After a short stay I then gave thanks to God for the safe arrival of the baby son and for answering prayer! I returned home on the bus to the centre of town and within two days the patient had died. They didn't ask for the funeral to be held at our Church, just across the road, as they were traditionally Catholics. I did of course attend the funeral and continued to visit the family afterwards.

Alberto had contact with several of the senior doctors in the hospital, partly I suppose because his brother was one of them. On a couple of occasions he got permission for the two of us to hand out New Testaments to the students as they left lectures at the Medical School. I also sometimes accompanied him as he went round talking to the doctors and handing them New Testaments. Those who were Communist sympathizers very much liked passages from the Epistle of James (Chapter 5 v.1 –6) condemning the rich for failing to pay just wages to their workers.

Some of the patients in the cancer foundation had some very drastic surgery and one Pentecostal patient I especially remember was one whose operation was fully successful. The surgeon, a very proud man of Spanish decent called D'Amesti, came round a few days later to find out how the patient was. 'How are you today then?" he asked. The patient replied 'Oh I'm completely healed – praise the Lord!' 'Praise who?' said the doctor. 'Who did the operation?'

One of the nursing sisters I got to know was a lecturer in the school of nursing. To my consternation one afternoon she asked me if I would give a brief lecture on psychology to the first year students! She commented that it would be easy as I had probably studied in seminary for five or six years! I tried to explain that whereas the

*Auxilary Nursing Training Course for Church members with their
Tutor, Maria Diaz, outside Renca Church. (1975)*

Roman Catholic priests had that length of training mine had been
nothing like that! She was very persistent and wouldn't be put off so
I thought it was another of those learning curves the Lord was placing
before me. He seemed to be doing that fairly often in those days so I
felt I had to agree! After some thought and prayer I rushed with all
haste to the Christian Literature Crusade bookshop in town. I was
fortunate enough to find a book in Spanish by Paul Tournier, a Swiss
doctor, in which he covered aspects of practical psychology.

Later the nurse invited me to visit some of her private cancer patients
in their homes. Being a Tutor sister at the hospital she later offered to
organise a short course in basic nursing for members of the Renca
congregation where I was Pastor. Quite a number of members were
unemployed so this provided an opportunity for them to work as
auxiliary nurses in private clinics. Most of them were mums whose
husbands were out of work, and seven of them acquired jobs at the
end of the course. Aunty Mary, as we nicknamed her, came to our
house occasionally and once gave Deborah a small nurse's cap and
apron.

New Arrival in the Family

During our last days at the Centre we had heard that a children's home in San Bernardo, near Santiago, was in need of a washing machine. There was a large very noisy one in the Centre that no one seemed to want. Preparing for everything to be cleared out of the Centre we arranged to take the machine to the children's home. We arrived and met Señora Juanita and Don Gregorio who were running the home. They were a very dedicated Christian couple. I can't remember exactly how many children there were in the home, but it was very much over subscribed, with probably sixty or seventy children there.

We noticed there was a very happy and loving atmosphere as we stood watching the children playing outside in the patio. One thing that impressed us enormously was how the bigger children were so good at caring for the smaller ones, and there was always such a wonderful family feeling. Señora Juanita was grateful for the slightly battered washing machine, and said it would help considerably with so many children's clothes to wash.

A year later returning from leave in England we visited the home again and Señora Juanita broached the subject of adoption. She was anxious to find Christian parents for three small children, one of whom was a baby about nine weeks old. Ann and I had thought about adopting a baby, but we hadn't really decided and I had assumed that if we did adopt it would obviously be a boy!

That afternoon we were shown into a small room where the babies were being cared for. Glancing round behind the door we saw one baby girl being carried in the arms of an older girl. I believe Ann then said something like 'There's a lovely baby!' at which moment the baby smiled at me! Half turning round I said to Ann "Yes she is lovely, if she answers to the sound of a teapot we'll have her!" This was the first time we

Stephen with his new sister (1974)

saw Elizabeth. Several weeks later Ann obtained the legal papers to make her Elizabeth's legal guardian.

I shall always remember the afternoon we were going to bring Elizabeth home. At one stage Peter and Stephen were talking on the back seat of the car. Stephen said 'What can you do with a baby sister; I mean you can't play with cars with her or anything!' However everything changed once we were on the way home and they became absolutely fascinated with her. When we stopped for an ice cream Stephen unexpectedly placed Elizabeth on his lap and offered her a lick of his ice cream! She had suddenly become an immediate success!

Later when we thought about baptism we asked Juanita and Gregorio to be Elizabeth's Chilean godparents. I was then Pastor of the Church at Renca so Elizabeth was the first of our own children that I actually baptised.

Chapter 13
COUP D'ÉTAT AND PRISON

There was hardly any food in the shops now with violence and hatred increasing every day! The country was becoming bankrupt and it was impossible to buy anything that had normally been imported. As most medical drugs came from abroad, and were paid for in dollars, only those produced in Chile were now prescribed. Unfortunately although they were a lot cheaper many of these were also inferior! Operating theatres in the hospitals were now often closed and patients were being sent home!

One morning in June the papers and the radio announced there had been an attempted coup. Two or three regiments of tanks had driven into the capital. However within a few hours they were made to withdraw. Yet many people, and especially housewives, were now putting the military under more and more pressure to intervene. People were just fed up with a government trying to force as many changes through as fast as possible. Instead of getting measures properly passed by parliament they were getting them through by decree. Many people felt that things had gone so far now that the country was in complete chaos. It was imperative that the Military moved in to protect the constitution, of which they were the guardians. Yet things were going to continue to deteriorate for several more months yet.

An English friend working in Santiago rang to say he had quite a lot of clothes sent out from England to be given to the poor. As he had no contact with the poorer people he asked me if I could use them. I agreed but being conscious I was a foreigner I felt it might be difficult for me to accurately assess each family's needs. So I asked some of the mums from the Renca Church if they would go with me, feeling they were better qualified to do that. We went out as a group in the Volkswagen stopping on the edge of each shantytown. The ladies first went into the homes and decided the needs of each family. They then came back to collect and distribute the clothes that they thought were most appropriate.

This same English friend invited Ann and I to lunch one day. The meal was egg salad because with no meat this was about the only protein you could get. He was well informed politically so I asked him what he thought would be the outcome of the present state of things. He reckoned 'Something was in the air and soon there would be shooting in the streets, but it wouldn't come to very much!' I told him how alarmed I was that people involved in peaceful demonstrations were being shot at from government offices in the Plaza behind the President's Palace. He made no comment so I still have a feeling that this friend was not going to tell me all he knew that day!

Finally one morning in September 1973 as I was listening to the radio before breakfast at 7.45 am President Salvador Allende began addressing the people. He was saying he was being hounded out of the Presidential palace. The military had given him several hours to leave and promised him safe passage in an aeroplane if he agreed. Defiantly he refused to comply and said the only way he would leave would be feet first! In the broadcast he told us he expected them to cut him off at any time and within minutes the radio went dead! At this point I immediately thought of some of his earlier words when he had said that arms would be given to the people when the time came! This remark had always scared me and although it never happened it was certainly something I had always worried about! Just before the President's speech that morning I had been reading part of Psalm 2. Reading the opening words again they seemed so appropriate for the occasion! 'Why do the nations conspire and the peoples plot in vain? The kings of the earth take their stand and the rulers gather together against the Lord. Therefore, you kings be wise; be warned you rulers of the earth. Serve the Lord with fear and rejoice with trembling. Kiss (i.e. worship) the Son lest he be angry and you be destroyed in your way' (v10-12).

It has been said that if the changes Allende's government had wanted to bring about had been introduced more slowly the Coup would probably never have happened. However having said that Allende's government was a coalition of different parties of the left. Some of the ministers in his government were much more radical than he was and wanted things to move even faster. One minister had insidiously infiltrated the Navy and attempted to get the senior ranks to mutiny and overpower the commissioned officers!

I waited for further news on the radio before leaving for work that morning. At last it was announced that people were to be off the streets by 1.00 pm and then remain indoors until further notice. I felt

164

it was important to report to the hospital. So on this occasion putting on my clerical collar (which I had never been expected to wear) I got down there quickly. This was the only time I found the metal gates actually shut, but the porters soon let me in. The Director thanked me for coming in, and I told her I would be available for anything she felt I could do. I imagined that there would probably be large numbers of casualties flooding into the hospital. It was a hot summer's morning with groups of patients at the Lopez Perez Cancer Foundation sitting outside enjoying the sunshine. They told me they had heard the news on the radio and that the Air Force was threatening to bomb the Presidential Palace if Allende refused to leave. I found this just incredible and in no way could I believe that this was possible and remember saying 'oh they can't possibly do that!'

My unbelief was soon to be tested because about 11.00 am several Hawker Hunters began circling the city centre. It felt a bit like sitting in the cinema waiting for the big picture to begin, filling me with a mixture of excitement and great apprehension. On this beautiful hot sunny day with blue sky as always there was an uncanny sense of uncertainty for no one could really imagine what would happen next. As I sat down on a low garden wall chatting to a patient I immediately saw a bent bullet. It was a spent ·303, one familiar to me from my Army days. Leaning over to pick it up I was too slow as one of the patients snapped it up as a souvenir. I have to say it reminded me so much of the larger shell caps we used to collect as schoolboys during the blitz. The Hunters were now circling close to the city centre when suddenly the noise of aero-engines was interrupted by several explosions. Then within minutes columns of black smoke began climbing into the sky. Rockets had been fired with some precision into the upper part of the Presidential Palace and soon the roof was on fire. Even as I stood watching the dark columns ascending into the sunshine it all seemed impossible to believe and still very like being in the cinema.

In less than an hour I decided I ought to go home, by which time all public transport was out of sight and the streets deserted. In some ways not all that different to what we had been forced to get used to. Each week we had seen fewer and fewer buses and coaches on the streets. Public transport was in a terrible state with broken down vehicles standing idle in the depots due to shortages of spares and lack of proper servicing.

On the way home that day many people were standing stranded by the bus stop near the hospital hoping for a bus to get them home. Fortunately the Volkswagen was now repaired and having eight seats I allowed people to clamber in. Until I realised we were being completely overloaded and had to jump out to shut the sliding door. Doing a bit of a detour I began dropping people off and eventually arrived back home just before 1.00 pm. It was almost like a public holiday except for the empty streets and uncanny silence. We had to remain indoors for two more days, and were then informed there would be a curfew every day between 11.00 pm at night and 7.00 am in the morning. The curfew was later made shorter and was brought forward to 6.00 am.

A few weeks later the Baptist Church decided they wanted their bungalow back so we moved again to another bungalow belonging to a German couple. Our new landlord owned a factory in Santiago. This time we were on a main road called Brown Norte in another residential borough of Santiago called Nuñoa. We were fascinated to find that we had an Arab family from Bethlehem on one side, and a Jewish family from Poland on the other. Within a few days our Jewish neighbours invited us in for drinks and refreshments. That evening we stayed several hours and of course forgot all about the curfew. Eventually realising we ought to go home we then became aware that we were not allowed to go out into the street! 'Ah why not climb over our back wall!' suggested our host! Consequently finding a ladder the boys went over first, followed by Ann and Deborah and I came last carrying Elizabeth. Once at the top of the wall we all clambered down into our own back garden on the other side!

Mr and Mrs Popovich were very friendly and we got on well with them. He had two old classic American cars; one was a Buick and the other a Plymouth. He said the running costs were minimal even though petrol had been so expensive, especially on the black market. From time he would ask me to call in and read to him from his English Bible. One evening I decided to call by to see him on the way home. Like most residential areas in the cities they had high metal railings outside the house and a high gate that was always kept locked. I rang the bell and one of their two maids came out. 'Unfortunately I'm afraid Mr Popovich is in bed.' the girl said. A couple of days later I called again and he came to the door himself. 'Are you better I'm sorry you were not well the other day?' I exclaimed. 'Oh I'm fine!' he replied 'You see I always stay in bed for Jewish festivals - I'm a Jew by tradition not by conviction!' I have often reflected on his words and think how like so many people in England who would consider themselves Christians, but certainly have very little conviction!

Food began coming back into the shops very quickly after the Coup. Potatoes had been in short supply and we found that two or three shiploads had been standing out at sea and had not been unloaded for some unknown reason. Bread soon appeared in the shops once again. I still find it absolutely unbelievable to think that a South American country – where bread is eaten virtually at every meal – had been without bread for so many weeks!

Because of all the shortages we had not been able to spend our money! In fact I had several wads of notes stashed away in a wardrobe drawer. Consequently just before the Coup we decided to buy an expensive guitar and a piano – both second hand - from missionaries who had decided to leave the country. I need to confess that because we couldn't spend our money on essentials we became the first Anglican missionaries to purchase a television! It had been advertised in a national daily paper, and the man selling it said he had three that had been given to him in payment of a debt. They were completely new and still in their packaging and cardboard boxes. At the time I somehow thought his story seemed a bit fishy but felt a television was a good investment. Since then I have a horrible suspicion that we may have inadvertently bought our television on the Black Market! In the midst of all the turmoil the latter had been thriving under the Allende Government. A theatre down town was found jam-packed with consumer goods like refrigerators, washing machines and cookers; all of which had not been seen in the shops for a very long time. Petrol was also offered to me at five times the normal price, which I just refused to pay on principle!

We used to put a tablecloth over the television when we had prayer meetings – because we were too embarrassed to admit to being so worldly. There was another reason we bought it though, and that was because it was so useful for keeping us up to date with the news. There were so many demonstrations, shootings, and explosions happening each day! At one stage we telephoned the British Embassy to find out what plans they had for us if civil war broke out! We were told that we could come to the Embassy but there were certainly no plans to get us to the airport, or get us out of the country!

A few weeks before the Coup some English speaking friends, we had met on the ship leaving England, called by to see us. They had a large brand new Citroen car with a Kalashnikov reclining on the back seat which the husband explained 'was to protect them because there was so much shooting going on!' I honestly couldn't see the need for such a sophisticated sub-machine gun and I began to wonder what they were up to? Peter and Stephen however seemed much more interested in their superb car, whose suspension rose up when the ignition was turned on. Later at the time of the Coup the wife arrived at our house in a very distressed state saying that the military intended to arrest her and had attempted to rape her maid! She told us she had left the house leaving her children with friends. Soon after this we discovered our telephone was bugged. The husband had previously worked in Cuba and had, as he put it, 'been involved in the agricultural revolution there'. Like so many things we only knew part of the story and didn't know what they were really doing in Chile! Certainly lots of foreign nationals had entered Chile since the Allende government had come to power.

During Allende's presidency hundreds of Cuban doctors flooded into Chile. It was explained to me that this was because of a shortage of Chilean medics! Other people I talked to were unhappy with this infiltration because the Cubans had been given a year's less training than Chilean doctors. Another thing that caused me concern was when the President announced that all foreigners would soon be put out of the country. I assumed this had been said with factory owners and businessmen in mind, so that the government could continue to take over the nationalisation of privately owned industries. However I didn't really know so this was another statement that added to my feelings of fear and insecurity.

Curfew-Breaking!
After the Coup I continued to go across town on Sundays to the evening service at Renca. Returning home one night as usual I caught the bus from Church to the Plaza de Armas by the central Post Office. Normally from here I would get a second bus home. Strangely this night I found the last bus had already gone! I hung around for some time hoping to get a taxi or something but eventually

realised I was stranded! I had no idea how I would get home, so eventually pulling myself together I decided I had no other option than to walk! The main problem was not transport but the curfew! So from the Plaza de Armas, I walked along towards Alameda Avenue. Soon street lamps were going out and the traffic had already stopped. Looking up as I walked I could see people peering at me from their upstairs windows over the shops. Twenty minutes later the streets were deserted and plunged into complete darkness. Not wanting to give the impression I wanted to hide in the shadows I decided it was best to walk down the middle of the road. I kept going for some time, up to the Plaza Italia, along Avenida Providencia, and continued along Apoquindo. Turning right along Tobalaba, where the canal runs along by the road, I was only about half a mile from home. It was now well past the curfew time and I was drawing near to the main trolley bus depot. So with a sigh of relief I began to think to myself 'It won't be long now I'm almost home!' As it was still so extremely dark I decided I would continue to walk down the middle of the road. Then all at once I noticed a movement in the shadows to my right and I saw an armed policeman standing by a tree. He immediately shouted 'Halt' and striding to the middle of the road swung around to face me. I then watched as he quietly and deliberately slipped the safety catch off his semi-automatic rifle! I felt a shiver go down my spine but there was no point in trying to run, there was nowhere to go! Although I was overwhelmed with fear I felt I must try to be calm.

Then to my surprise I saw a second armed Carabinero standing silently in the shadows ready to shoot me. 'What's in that bag?' the first man asked. I stood still and speaking as calmly as I possibly could, said 'I'm a Pastor returning from Church, and the bag contains a Bible and a Hymn Book.' I quickly added I had missed the last bus home and only lived down the next road about 300 metres from the corner where we were standing. 'Open the bag slowly!' he continued. I then began to sense that possibly he was more scared than I was! Unfortunately this began to make me feel more scared than ever. He was possibly thinking I have a bomb or explosives in the bag? 'Take the books out slowly one by one and hold them up!' he said. Anxiously wanting to comply I tried tremulously to hold them up as high as I could for several very long seconds! Then quite unexpectedly and to my enormous relief he said 'O.K. on your way!'

I wanted to run - but without daring to look back and with as much dignity as I could muster - I walked down to unlock the front gate. Striding through the front garden I then slowly opened the front door slipping in as silently as possible! Standing with my back to the wall I was trembling from head to foot!

An American Baptist Pastor who had children in the school where ours attended had a similar experience. He was a typical Texan with a couple of large pickup trucks who liked to do things in a big way! Like all of us he needed to go to the local police station to obtain permission to hold some Church meeting or other. In his usual flamboyant fashion he drove up to the station, slammed on the breaks, leapt out of his vehicle and began striding up to the entrance. Suddenly a loud voiced sergeant screamed 'Halt!' The American froze on the spot and stood straddled like a statue. After a long pause slowly several pale faced policemen began peering out of the station windows! Later the sergeant informed our Texan friend that if he had not stopped when ordered to do so he would have been riddled with bullets! The sallow faced sergeant continued 'Don't ever do that again – you scared the living daylights out of us!' A couple of days later I became aware of the reason why the policemen had been so scared. Reading the newspapers I discovered that during the past week a number of police stations had been bombed or had had explosives thrown into them!

Visiting the Prisoners

Some time after the Coup I had a phone call from the English friend who had invited us to the egg salad lunch. He told me that apart from military personnel held there were a number of other prisoners in "Los Capuchinos". The buildings were part of an old school belonging to the Roman Catholic Church taken over by the military as a temporary prison after the Coup, and not far from the centre of Santiago. My friend then said 'certain of the detainees are members of the acting fraternity and people I know well – could you possibly visit them?' I assured him that I would do my very best to visit them if the authorities allowed me to.

Later I discovered that other Pastors had heard about this detention centre and three or four of us gathered outside early one morning. We were kept waiting for some time and were finally let in one at a time. I was ushered into an office and discovered I was to be interviewed by a retired colonel. He looked very stern, and without asking me to sit down, asked me why I wanted to visit the prisoners. With stiff upper lip and staring through horned rimmed spectacles I got the idea he was trying to scare me. To my great surprise it would seem he'd never heard of the Anglican Church. So I plucked up courage and gave him a little lecture about the medical, educational and social work carried out by Anglican missionaries over the past hundred years. I explained that in the nineteen thirties we had between 30 and 40 rural schools in Southern Chile, plus two hospitals, and several clinics for the indigenous people. He also needed to know that the Rev William Wilson, and Nurse Dorothy Royce had both been honoured by the Chilean government and been awarded gold medals for their work. So still staring at me in a serious military manner and without further questions he said 'Well I need a reference from your superior and after fifteen days we will let you know!' On request David Pytches told me he was happy to give me a letter but warned 'be careful, and if you get yourself locked up ring me and I'll come and get you out!' After about three weeks I discovered that our friend Captain Alex Hughes and I were the only two Pastors granted passes. So at first we began visiting together but later we went separately once the guards had got to know us.

The school consisted of large classrooms with high ceilings, and there were a number of single storey open sided workshops in the patio at the back. The front of the building was approached from the main street across a forecourt and past a security office. Inside there was a large hall with benches where visitors could sit and talk to their relatives. Once inside I was allowed to wander freely around the workshops amongst the prisoners, many of whom were technicians. Some seemed able to repair almost anything from old radios to saucepans, whilst others preferred working in leather or wooden goods. The prisoners were mainly senior Non Commissioned Officers in the forces. Amongst other prisoners was a group of some twelve professional actors. They were kept apart and were not found in the workshops and seemed very pleased to see me. I mentioned the person who had asked me to come and they talked to me mainly about their wives and families. When they gave me their addresses I promised to go and visit them.

Alex Hughes and I asked if we might lead a weekly Bible study and permission was granted. It seemed a sensible way of meeting the men and hopefully of giving them some encouragement. Those who came were mainly military personnel. At first they eyed me with great suspicion obviously wondering why I had come to visit them. I was fairly sure this might happen. So having introduced myself I went on to say that it was not the authorities, or even the Church that had asked me to come, but I believed God wanted me to visit them. The second week, in order to get to know them, I suggested that I pass round a sheet for them to write their names on! This was not a good idea as some thought there was an ulterior motive here! However they eventually accepted the fact that I only wanted to try to remember their names and they seemed a bit more relaxed afterwards!

At the beginning we were all under tight supervision. Orders were that the Chapel doors were to be left wide open so that the guards could see that nothing subversive was going on inside. I was somewhat surprised when I first looked out through the Chapel doors. For sitting opposite on a balcony was a guard with a heavy machine gun pointing at me. It certainly helped to concentrate the mind, but I am not certain to this day whether he would have actually fired it or not! Maybe it was just to instil fear, I shall never know!

One week someone asked us what was hell like? Alex answered by saying 'Hell is the place where God is not. A place where only those who had experienced the love of God would never want to go to!' We decided to study the life of Christ in the Gospels, as we thought this would be the least controversial. At the end of each study the men asked questions. One nineteen year old, who was in the Navy, asked me why we had said Jesus had never used violence. He went on to quote Jesus' act of cleansing the temple saying surely he had used some violence when casting out the people who sold doves and animals, and those changing money? Good question! I was at first stumped but then encouraged him to look at the Bible passage with me. It then became clear that although Jesus had formed a whip to drive out the animals there is no record of him using this on the traders! After that I asked him about his family, and was later able to visit his parents who lived just outside Valparaiso. They were so glad that I had actually seen their son and was able to tell them he was well. Before leaving they thanked me for taking the trouble to make a round journey of some 120 miles to see them.

One week after the bible study another man with a handle bar moustache – obviously in the Air Force – said he was interested in becoming ordained. But as he was divorced did I think that would be a problem for the Anglican Church? I answered him by saying that he needed first of all to know Jesus personally - and I didn't tackle the issue of ordination! One week when Colin Bazley was in Santiago he was able to accompany me. After the Bible study one of the men asked with some feeling "Why did God allow so much evil in the world?" Colin replied 'Why blame God for that? Who causes most of the conflicts and wars in the world?'

One extremely worried man told me that now as he had no income his mortgage payments were getting in serious arrears. His was fearful that this would mean his wife and children might soon be evicted from the family home. I called to see his wife and two small daughters and later got his mortgage payments reduced. Working at the same time in the hospital was a great advantage, for the social workers would give me advice regarding some of the prisoners' problems.

As I visited some of the families they wondered who I was, and treated me with extreme suspicion, but this was usually quickly overcome. One prisoner told me his wife had just had their first child and he had not been able to see his wife or baby. His wife was staying with his parents. So once he had given me the address I went to visit her and was able to reassure him that all was well. Ann gave them some baby clothes afterwards. Another man said he was divorced but his ex-wife was very supportive and was still standing by him. Ann and I got to know her and she came to our home several times. Their little boy was a bright little lad, extremely hyper active and quite a handful. The wife was an actress and got work doing television commercials to support the family financially whilst the husband was in prison.

After some time I discovered there were other political prisoners in the main prison in Santiago near Mapocho railway station. In fact there were more members of the acting fraternity there as well. One day a Roman Catholic Priest invited me to accompany him on his visit to this prison. Having taken me through the main security barrier he left me in an open patio and several men came to chat with me. These prisoners told me that it was agreed with the authorities that if they could get work contracts outside the country arrangements could be made to extradite them. Before leaving the prison that day they gave me letters to post with applications for jobs abroad enclosing their Identity Cards.

The men also asked me if they could have their correspondence sent to my address. They explained that they no longer trusted the authorities as some of their letters had got lost and their Identity Cards had gone missing! After this I used to post the men's letters for them and brought them the correspondence that arrived in my post box marked for them. Several of them received replies offering them short film contracts in Canada, Germany, Great Britain and countries prepared to take political refugees.

On my visits to the Mapocho prison I continued to chat with groups of the men in the patio. Some would then ask me to read their letters and translate them into Spanish for them. On one hot summer's afternoon I was reading the prisoners letters aloud in the patio when a shout echoed across from the guards! Then rushing across the patio they bellowed I was breaking prison rules! 'You're reading documents in a foreign language and that's against the regulations here' they shouted! Shrugging my shoulders I replied that the letters were written in English and I was just translating them so the men could understand! However they repeated I was breaking the rules, and then grabbing me by the elbows frog marched me away! I have to confess I quickly began to think of those words of David Pytches when he had said 'If you get yourself locked up, just ring me and I'll come and get you out!' Fortunately once out of the patio they just asked me to leave the prison. I did however continue to visit this particular prison afterwards but I was never allowed to read the prisoners letters out loud to them again.

On another occasion the guards at the Mapocho prison entrance confiscated a pile of Bibles I was taking in. I was a bit put out as I had previously done this for the weekly Bible study at Los Capuchinos. 'Why are you doing that?' I protested! 'Well some people have been bringing in books with the middle cut out with things concealed inside!' the guard explained. His reason really astonished me but I suppose it was possibly plausible! So taking the Bibles back one at a time I proceeded to thumb through them page by page to show him there was nothing inside and he finally let me take them in.

At Los Capuchinos the guards were getting to know me and were more relaxed. One week, knowing some of the prisoners were technicians, I took in a small Japanese tape recorder. I had tried unsuccessfully to get this repaired at the shop where I bought it, so I thought perhaps one of the men might be able to fix it. Sadly it was beyond repair but as I was leaving with it under my arm one of the guards stopped me. 'What do you have there?' he asked. On learning it was a tape recorder he said "Oh you shouldn't have brought that in, it could have been be used to smuggle in messages!" I apologised profusely saying the idea had never occurred to me. However the guard didn't confiscate it and he seemed quite unconcerned about it!

From Eviction to House Church

Things were gradually beginning to get better in the hospital – at least all the political demonstrations and strikes had finished. One afternoon a senior nursing sister approached me in the corridor of the Lopez Perez Foundation. Unbeknown to me she said she had previously disapproved of my sense of humour. Because she said 'when ever you come into a ward people are always falling about laughing and there is always so much noise!' She was a dedicated nurse of the old school in her sixties who had worked for many years in the Cancer Foundation. Since the Coup she had become extremely worried about her brother who was a doctor, as he with others had been an Allende supporter. 'Now he is under suspicion by the military' she told me. It looked likely that her brother might lose his job. 'Would you pray for him please' she asked. I promised that I would and to my knowledge her brother kept his post.

Another day an auxiliary nurse in the Chest Hospital spoke to me. As we walked along the corridor she told me she needed to speak to me in confidence. Outside in the grounds she said 'my brother has been imprisoned by the Military, would you have time to visit my sister-in-law?' She felt she must warn me that there had previously been a lot of shooting in the neighbourhood where they lived. To my relief on arrival I found no roadblocks and no police in sight, so I parked the Mission Volkswagen in a street nearby. The sister-in-law lived in a terraced house in a fairly unpretentious area and she answered the door.

Inside one wall was completely lined with books and I discovered that her husband had worked as a journalist for Allende. Her voice was very weak and speaking quietly she told me she was suffering from severe tuberculosis, was coughing up blood and wasn't eating very much. Her greatest concern was for her two teenage children – a girl and a boy. They were getting on well with their studies at school but there was little money for food or essentials. In fact she was selling off the furniture bit by bit to pay for food. In addition to this she wanted to visit her husband but could not afford the fare! I was able to leave her some rice and sugar with some money for other needs. I also gave her enough money to pay her fare to Valparaiso and back and promised I would call again. I also pleaded with her not to sell any more furniture because without their dad it was essential that the children should at least have the comforts of the family home! As I was about to leave she then blurted out 'Anyway the owner of the house wants to evict us as soon as possible!' I asked if she had a Bible amongst all their books, read a few verses, and asked if I could pray with them. She confessed that she had no personal faith in God but thanked me for coming. I called twice more, and she seemed a little better, and I gave her some more food and money. The last time I went to visit her neighbours told me she had moved away and I lost contact with her.

However the Lord was still at work and some months later, whilst having the evening meal at home, the phone rang. 'It's Mrs Klopping – do you remember me?' What I heard next was incredible! 'Some kind friends have acquired a site for me, and others have given me money to build a small house. I want to thank you for your help and to ask you to come to see me because I want to start a Church in my house!' 'Do you remember saying "You must trust the Lord for He will provide for you!"' Yes, I did remember because the last time she had spoken to me she asked if I could get her a large sum of money to build a house. I had felt thoroughly miserable because after consulting with my Bishop I had to say to her 'I am sure you will feel I am a complete failure and have let you down, but we can't provide that amount of money.' Yes I had also added 'Trust the Lord, He will not let you down!' Now this was absolutely incredulous news! However I had to explain that I could not come. Within a few days we were returning to England because my father was ill, but I was sure others would help start the Church in her house!

Chapter 14
LIFE AFTER THE COUP

My parents decided to come out to Chile for Christmas in 1973. On one lovely sunny morning my dad and I were chatting on the patio. Dad told me he had been under going further hospital treatment. He continued that if things didn't clear up he would probably need another operation. I remember it well because I had tried to persuade my parents not to come. At the time we were living a few blocks from a Military Non Commissioned Officers training school. Although it was three months since the Coup groups of Allende supporters continued attacking the school. For weeks, night after night, we could hear loud bursts of firing going on!

Around the time the authorities had been searching for a suspect not far from us in Santiago and had discovered a man with gun shot wounds. I need to say here that the law in Chile has always demanded that if a doctor or nurse treats someone in such a condition this must be reported to the police. Doctor Sheila Cassidy had unfortunately treated the wounded man and had failed to report it. During this search the authorities had also shot and killed a priest accidentally. Later we were appalled to read in a Times report that Sheila Cassidy had not just been arrested, but also tortured. This was the first time we had actually read about the work of D.I.N.A. (the secret police) who had been doing this sort of thing to so many people.

With things like this happening I tried hard to persuade my parents not to come out because the security situation was a long way off from normal. Dad in his usual positive way had responded by saying 'Well that shouldn't affect us too much; our main purpose is to have time with you and the children!' He had already hinted his health had not been so good and they were really looking forward to seeing us all.

For some time following the Coup people were still not allowed to hold any Church services, bible studies or public meetings. The Military still didn't know which people to trust and clandestine meetings were going on in some Churches. One well known left wing Presbyterian Pastor, whom it was said was going to be Allende's

Minister of Religion, was holding meetings in a room at the back of a Church not far from our home. Eventually when things quietened down religious services were allowed once again but only on recognised Church premises. Even then any meeting held in private houses - such as prayer meetings or Bible studies - needed official permission. Yet against this backdrop the Church at Renca where I was Pastor was thriving!

At this time brothers Eliseo and José Ortiz, the lay leaders of our Church decided that we should begin some half nights of prayer. The problem was there was no way of getting home during the curfew, so people would have to stay indoors until the end of the curfew. As I lived nearer to the centre of town I was told to make the necessary application for a permit. I turned up at the Ministry of Defence and spoke to a young lance corporal. He explained the procedure was that I had to write to the Military Commander of the Region of Santiago asking for permission. I returned to hand in the type-written letter when to my astonishment was reprimanded by a lieutenant. He informed me I had not spelt the commanding officer's name correctly and would have to go away and rewrite the letter. I was beginning to feel they were stalling me, and I was losing patience with them. Objecting strongly I responded that it wasn't my fault. 'That was how the lance corporal told me to write it, and when I was a clerk in the Army I was expected to know how to spell properly!' But I needed to hold my cool otherwise I wouldn't get the necessary permit! I must also say that to be fair the youngster was only a conscript and he possibly couldn't spell very well anyway.

A few days later I collected the said permission. From there I went to the local Police Station in Renca for them to countersign it, and was told to return in forty-eight hours. Once collected our copy of the permit then had to be carefully kept and shown to the authorities if they came to the house during the meeting. I found this all so time wasting, tedious and tiring. Eventually we could now hold the all night prayer meeting at the house next to the Church. Once the prayer meeting was under way I asked Eliseo where the permit was. 'Oh we went to the Police Station but it wasn't ready so we didn't trouble to go back to collect it!" He responded! I was absolutely speechless - and frightened – however they weren't bothered and the meeting went well!

This was my first experience of an all night prayer meeting. What actually happened was that during the night when people became very tired they would bed down in the house. The following morning once the curfew was over, and without waiting for breakfast, I dropped some of the members off on my way home.

God Answers Prayer

One day a lady in the Church approached me and pleaded with me to get her son out of prison! I listened carefully and understood that he had been accused of something he had certainly not done. I didn't really know how to begin so intended ringing the Bishop to see if we could engage a solicitor. I don't think that happened if I remember correctly. However some days later we had another night of prayer, and of course we prayed for the young man. Around nine o'clock whilst the meeting was in progress there was a knock at the door. This time we actually had the written permit on the mantelpiece. Thinking the authorities were probably checking up on us I slowly and fearfully opened the door. To my astonishment there was the lady's son standing on the doorstep! 'They've sent me home and dropped the charges' he said quietly!

At Renca on Sunday evenings Eliseo and José would lead singing before the service or meeting began. One played accordion and the other guitar. Getting off the bus you could hear the singing down the street encouraging people to come as the service was soon to begin. Bernadette (a young mum) probably about nineteen came in on one evening. Seeing lots of young people obviously enjoying themselves provoked a somewhat grumpy reaction from her. Turning on them she said 'what are you all looking so happy about?' 'Because Jesus loves us, and has forgiven our sins!' they responded. 'Does he love me then?' she retorted. 'Of course!' came their reply. Bernadette began coming to Church regularly and over a short period was changed, and she became a Christian.

On Saturday evenings there was usually a lively young people's meeting. One evening Bernadette was chatting with the young people and one of them asked her where's your husband? She explained that he had just lost his job and was staying at home with the baby. Later we discovered that he was suffering from severe arthritis and was unable to work. José suggested we go to visit him at the end of the meeting. Their small new timber house was just across from the

Church. It consisted of a one-roomed dwelling with a white sheet dividing the bedroom from the living room. On the floor was a kerosene stove, used mainly for cooking, but providing a little warmth for the baby's sake. Marcos was pleased to see the three of us and explained that the arthritis was made worse because he worked in the refrigeration part of a large super-market. His doctor had said he would never get better all the time he worked there! José suggested we lay hands on him and pray and he was quite willing for us to do so. The following day was Sunday and arriving at Church early I was surprised to see Bernadette with Marcos and the baby altogether sitting in Church. Marcos beamed at me – and so after greeting him I said 'now what's brought you here? – you must tell me about it.' Following the service I discovered the Lord had performed a miracle!

The night before after we left his house Marcos decided he wouldn't wait for his wife to come home and so went to bed. At about 1.00 am he awoke and felt a dull pain in his arm as if he had been given an injection. He got back into bed and slept until a few minutes before nine. Thinking it was getting late he quickly jumped out of bed and put the kettle on. Then he thought 'I jumped out of bed and I'm not in pain, and my arthritis has gone - I can't believe it - I've been healed!' The couple were overwhelmed with joy and Marcos became a Christian – and later I had the privilege of baptising them both and their baby.

Things continued to be difficult and sometimes the authorities would descend on the housing estates like Renca at six in the morning, and make all the men file out to the football pitch near the Church. The soldiers then searched them and made them lie on the ground, face down with hands behind their heads. Then suddenly the military would tell them to get up, go home and get off to work!

One Sunday evening I was on the bus going to Church. Approaching Renca the bus was stopped and the authorities came on board asking for identity cards. Going to my pocket I suddenly realised I hadn't got mine with me! I frantically searched through all my pockets, and then began to imagine what was going to happen next. Coming down the bus two young policemen were within three seats from me. Then unexpectedly to my utter amazement one called to his colleague and quickly turning round they got off the bus.

As I was working during the week in the hospital, and the Church was right across town, I didn't usually go to activities on weekdays except the Wednesday Bible Study. Eliseo and José decided that it was right to have a campaign and engaged two Pentecostal Pastors to conduct a series of meetings. Turning up on the last evening of the campaign I was introduced to these two gentlemen. After a brief conversation they told me seven young men had been converted and should be baptised. 'We understand that in your Church you only baptise by sprinkling' they said. 'But our custom is to baptise by immersion, so we are rather concerned!' they exclaimed. Wanting to come up with the right answer, and being afraid the new converts might go off to another Church, I frantically asked the Lord for wisdom! Then almost as if the words weren't mine I said 'Well what do you really think is the most important thing about baptism – is it water or the Holy Spirit?' 'Ah it's the Holy Spirit of course!' they replied, and the problem was resolved! The young men were very keen that I should baptise them as soon as possible. But I had to explain it was winter, and we always baptised people in the open air in the river. Then one of them said 'But you said once that if there were exceptional circumstances you might hire an indoor swimming pool for the occasion!" I suppose they were right but I wished they hadn't remembered it!

Eliseo baptising with Bernadette at top laughing.

So I made enquiries and in the end the only place had to be the Y.M.C.A. in the centre of town. The officials said that they normally only hired the pool to members – but finally agreed to let us use it. Yet our problems were not over for on the Saturday morning of the baptisms the street water main was being repaired. The water was cut off and the pool at best was only going to be half full! What a challenge to faith – but in no way could I let these seven young men down. The baptisms were on – and the congregation turned up with Rev Alf Cooper whom I had asked to preach. Eliseo, José and I all changed into our bathing trunks, and one of the pool stewards explained we must pass through the shower first and wash our feet. I remember asking him rather facetiously whether we did this before putting on our surplices or afterwards! Despite this he was very interested in what we were about to do and asked the young men lots of questions.

I think the young pool attendant was probably a Jehovah's Witness. I heard later that as a consequence of the baptisms he began attending the Church at Renca and became a Christian. Public Baptism is good a way to show the world that we want to follow Christ, and nearly always causes those who watch to think about where they stand concerning Jesus. The water was less than a metre deep, but there was enough. After waiting for swimmers to finish their time trials, and clear the pool, our short service was soon over. Later one of the new converts, who was a student, painted a picture of the sea off Viña del Mar, which was presented to me by the Church in Renca as a leaving present and we now have it in our hall way.

Other opportunities began to open up at the hospital and other members of staff came to our house for Bible study. Magali brought her husband Edgardo and Norma another social worker also came. The ladies were very open and took part with enthusiasm. Edgardo, a staunch Roman Catholic, tended to be argumentative and would often quote what he said was in the Bible. When challenged he said his problem was that he was short sighted and couldn't find the place! Our problem was that no one else could find the verses either because what he said was only his own version of what he thought was in the Bible! He also disagreed with passages that spoke of Jesus' brothers – insisting that Jesus didn't have any. However Magali had been wonderfully converted and continued to witness to patients and staff in the hospital where she worked.

Renca congregation. Eliseo with scarf, Florentino on right next to Ann. (1998)

Maximo Cheuquelaf with his wife Hilda, and three daughters. His son was at work. (1998)

Personal Encounters after the Coup

After the coup large numbers of those suspected of being Allende supporters were arrested. The military said they were determined to eradicate "this cancer of communism". One afternoon, when I wasn't at the hospital, I received a telephone message saying a Military personage wanted to call to see me at home if I would be in. Later a chauffeur driven staff car drew up near our house and a smartly dressed man in civilian suit came to the door. He turned out to be a retired Colonel and I invited him into the lounge. He had heard of me and said he was deeply worried about his son who had been imprisoned by the military. He was living at home with his parents and during a house to house search the military found an automatic rifle in a box under his bed. His father assured me the weapon was new and had never been used. Politely he asked 'Could I possibly help get the son out of prison as he was completely innocent of any armed opposition to the authorities?' As I sat listening and wondering what to say a knock came on the glazed lounge door from our hallway. Stephen opened the door and seeing I had a visitor, apologised for intruding in perfect Spanish and said "Excuse me Sir could I possible speak to my father please". I can't remember what Stephen's request was, but afterwards the Colonel said how impressed he was with my son, and what a polite young man he was! I later went to see the Lutheran Bishop, as I had heard he might be able to help. When I mentioned the name of the Colonel's son the Bishop smiled and remarked 'The person you speak of is one of the most wanted men in the country – whatever makes you think we can get him out?'

On another occasion a man came to see me whose sister worked in the hospital and had suggested I might be able to help. He owned a large egg cooperative and found one of his drivers had been swindling him. As the driver made his deliveries he was selling his own eggs to the customers instead of the cooperative ones. The owner had alarmingly discovered that through this man the firm was losing both large sums of money and customers. He challenged the driver and eventually felt he had no alternative but to sack him. Although he was very reluctant to do this as he had previously helped the man and put his confidence in him. He also knew that once sacked the driver would find it almost impossible to get another job. Unfortunately in retaliation the driver told the police that his boss was a former communist and was working against the military! The boss was obviously fearful that he would soon be arrested, and that his whole business would then collapse! Looking absolutely dejected he said to me 'I really don't know whom I can trust anymore, and I'm losing my faith!' I took him to mean faith in the people who worked for him. He seemed a little better for having talked to me, although I felt helpless to know how to help him! He was probably a nominal Roman Catholic, so I assured him I could identify with his feeling about people, and urged him not to lose his faith in the Lord!

I think this gives you some idea of what was going on after the Coup. I have to say that I never saw evidence of people being tortured or killed by the military. Of course many people were arrested and imprisoned for just being Allende sympathisers. Many reports have since been written in the press telling of torture that are true and have caused great distress. I have only attempted to talk of some people and situations that I know about personally.

There was just one occasion when returning home after a Confirmation service one Sunday evening in Renca we saw a body lying in the river. It was just before dark and several people walked down to the water's edge under a bridge where the man's body was lying in shallow water. But he was gone by the following evening. My account is just an attempt to talk about every day life during a very difficult and tumultuous time, which I pray Chile may never have to go through again. Doctor Salvador Allende's Marxist coalition assumed office in 1970 and soon attempted to polarize the country into Left and Right wing camps. The social and economic chaos of this government only finally began to subside with his overthrow and death on 11th September 1973.

Running for Joy

One of my lasting impressions of Santiago is of a man I used to see preaching in the main Plaza, opposite a large Catholic Church, by the Central Post Office. He was dressed in blue denim overalls and working boots, and was obviously on his way home from work. He was different to the normal Pentecostal preacher who spoke in the open air or on street corners, this man actually ran on the spot as he preached turning round as he did so that everyone could hear him. At first I thought this man is a bit over the top and tended to ignore him. Then one day I happened to meet someone who told me the man's story. He had worked as a mechanic in a garage for some years, but sadly fell ill, became paralysed and was confined to bed. Members of a local Pentecostal Church who lived nearby often used to pass by his house as they returned from work. One day they spoke to the man's wife and were concerned to find that he was so ill. 'Would you like us to come and pray with him?' they asked. She replied that she would have to ask him first as he wasn't a believer and might be offended! Going upstairs his wife passed on the message and he replied with some indifference "Well I don't see that it can do any harm."

So the visitors went upstairs, and standing around the bed prayed for the husband. Nothing happened, but these faithful people continued to call to pray on their way home from work for about six weeks. Then one day the wife went upstairs after they had left and found her husband sitting on the side of the bed. Within a few days strength returned to his body and he was able to return to work. He was so overjoyed now that he wanted to show the world that the Lord had healed him. He began avidly reading his Bible and later in the evenings started preaching in the Plaza de Armas. He wanted so much to demonstrate the new physical strength the Lord had given him that he always preached running on the spot! He often preached quoting the words of John the Baptist on repentance, which he had learned from memory. I have seen others try to copy him, but no one could do it with his genuine uniqueness! I love the notice I used to see when I took my shoes to be repaired in a little cobbler's off the Alameda. 'Difficult things we do immediately, the impossible takes a bit longer!' A good thing to keep in mind when you are praying!

Losing one's Marbles!
Because of my dad's ill health and the possibility of a pending operation I felt I must now return to England. Preparing to pack up we soon found it was impossible to get insurance cover for things like cameras, electrical equipment etc. So we decided to sell most of these things off cheaply to friends and use the money to buy new ones once back in England. Our three younger children, Stephen, Deborah, and Elizabeth, all needed their Chilean passports renewed so we had to go down town to what was called the office of 'Investigations' To get in the queue we had to leave at 5.30 am in the morning even though the curfew was still in force until 6.00 am. This

meant leaving home whilst it was still dark. So before leaving the house we had to stick a white flag out of the car window, to conform with curfew regulations just in case the authorities stopped us. We managed to park near the offices and got into the queue further along the block.

During the past few months Stephen had become very competent at marbles, and insisted on taking a large bag containing several hundred everywhere he went! Whilst we all stood in the queue on that dark morning before dawn suddenly the string broke. Soon the scene was something akin to a Charlie Chaplin film. The marbles were suddenly cascading onto the pathway and spreading out like giant hail stones right across the pavement. At once people walking by, and people in the queue, were slipping and sliding and falling flat on their backs! One or two people thought this was funny but we were so embarrassed. We did our best to pick them up and one or two kind folks helped us! After another hour's wait we were fortunate to be amongst the hundred people allowed to enter the building that day. But unbelievably Stephen once more managed to spill the contents of his bag all over the wooden floor in the corridor. Much to the delight of fellow document seekers and to the annoyance of 'Investigations' officials! Our faces were extremely red!

Homeward Bound

A few days later on board ship our documents were inspected for the last time. We were asked how much money in dollars we were taking out of the country. I replied at a guess something like five hundred, to which the official responded that we were over our limit and breaking regulations. Fortunately he realised we were English, and when I explained that this money came from selling goods from our home he let us off! Some hours afterwards on deck we were relaxing as we moved away from the port of Valparaiso. At this point a friendly smartly dressed man came across and began chatting to Ann in a rather familiar manner. After a while Ann commented that although he seemed to know her - she didn't know who he was! He replied 'Ah well maybe not - actually I'm a doctor - but I was behind your family in the queue at the passport office on the morning your son upset all his marbles over the pavement!' The ship moved up the coast of Chile and as we were getting near to Antofagasta I looked back to see we were being shadowed by a Chilean naval destroyer. It was later rumoured that our ship, which was an Italian liner, could have been carrying arms and the Navy wanted to see us out of Chilean waters! The communists in Italy were very angry because the Coup had overthrown Allende's communist coalition government.

We were pleased to be travelling with Colin Bazley's parents who had been visiting Chile and were now returning to England. Disembarking in Panama we travelled by air to the United States spending a few days near Tampa in what was called "D and D Missionary Homes". Two retired American missionary ladies had wanted to provide accommodation for missionaries on leave who had nowhere to live. The site had between 30 and 40 units. Some were chalets but we were provided with a beautiful mobile home. It contained a large lounge, living room, several bedrooms, kitchen, full bathroom and toilet. They had even filled the fridge with food and fresh milk. All we were expected to pay was two dollars a day to help maintain the site and agree to do half-a-day's odd jobs helping the janitor. On the second day we were given free vouchers to go to 'the Missionary Barrel', which was like a small one storey department store. Here they kitted our family out with several sets of clothes and shoes. Most of the things were second hand, but were of a very high quality. I remember being given two lightweight suits and then saying I couldn't get everything in our cases. 'No problem' they said and produced another suitcase! We had so little money that we dare not tell the children we were only a few miles from Disneyland. The one outing we did have was to the local fire station where the boys were delighted to climb up into the Fire Engines and talk to the Fire Fighters. After two weeks we then went to stay in a friend's flat in Indianapolis whilst he was away. We got to know him when he was doing a doctorate in Chile and had attended the Centre congregation in Santiago.

By this time we had spent all our dollars! But as we walked through Chicago airport the children said they felt hungry, so quickly counting up I found we had just enough money to buy a hamburger each! During the long flight Stephen spent most of the night teaching a Jewish gentleman next to him how to play poker! Elizabeth was in a cot at the front of the seats on a shelf and when she became restless raised her legs up so that they were silhouetted on the screen for everyone to see them! My most embarrassing experience came whilst trying to listen to the film sound track for free. At the beginning of the flight a stewardess came round offering us headsets at some exorbitant price. Peter however had discovered that if you inserted a thick drinking straw into the arm socket of the seat it acted as effectively as the headphones. Following my ingenious son's advice, as I was trying to connect my improvised headset, to my great embarrassment a stewardess came along and caught me in the act!

Arriving back in England we were delighted that granddad's health had improved with medical treatment and the operation was put off. For the first few weeks we stayed with Ann's dad in St Alban's. Then after six weeks we moved into a house in South Harrow where I was to work as a Curate at Christ Church Roxeth. Three years later, and just before moving up to Nottinghamshire, granddad went into hospital and died of cancer of the pancreas. The medical people assured us that this was nothing to do with his previous cancer of the stomach. The Lord had taken care of him for nearly twenty-three years after that first life saving medical miracle and we would now stay in England to look after my mother.

The Lord still continues to give me new challenges and amaze me by the things He does through us. You don't have to be clever or have exceptional ability. The main lesson I've learnt is to listen to Him carefully and be obedient. If the Lord can use me He can use anyone to 'Give Glory to God'.

Elizabeth, Darren,
Sheila Baughan and
Ann. (1998)

Nivel Embarque

Lady Police Constable
at Pudahuel Santiago Airport
(1998)

From the right: Ziola, Ann, Zoila's mother, Zoila's niece
and daughter Alexandra standing. (1998).